LOST TOWNS OF NORTH CAROLINA

HEATHER LEAH

Published by The History Press
An imprint of Arcadia Publishing
Charleston, SC
www.historypress.com

Cover image courtesy of Anita Brittain.

First published 2026

Manufactured in the United States

ISBN 9781467159791

Library of Congress Control Number: 2025948407

With much love to my mom, dad, and husband,
who believed in me and helped my dream come true.

CONTENTS

INTRODUCTION

Many people, myself included, have a fascination with ghost towns. There's something eerie and surreal about standing in the middle of a community whose time has passed—hollow houses tipping sideways with decay, wrapped like mummies in overgrown ivy and weeds. There was once a time, long ago, when this haunting house was somebody's cozy home. It was the safe place where children were raised, where happy memories were made. Families ate dinner here. They went to work each day and then, at night, sat around the fireplace and shared stories with loved ones.

What was life like when this ghost town was still in its heyday?

How did a once-thriving community become not only abandoned—but forgotten by the outside world?

And if this town, once so full of life, could be completely wiped off the map, could my own hometown someday be a ghost town, too?

Ghost towns and lost communities can be found all across North Carolina, if you know where to look. They're hidden off hiking trails in the woods of state parks. They're tucked away down winding rural roads, sitting high on the mountains, and isolated on abandoned islands. Some are even completely submerged underwater. In fact, it's likely you've driven past a ghost town and not even realized it.

Some of the state's ghost towns date back to the 1700s, older than the United States itself. Some were bustling port towns with immense amounts of wealth; others were humble mill villages. Each town had its own personality, with some full of rabble-rousers who literally sparked the Revolutionary War and others full of peace-keepers who risked everything to help freedom seekers on the Underground Railroad.

How Does an Entire Town Get Destroyed?

Even with incredible connections to colonial and antebellum history, none of these towns were saved. Some were destroyed quickly, under cannon fire in the rage of war, or devastated by acts of God and Mother Nature. Others were choked out slowly, left behind as the world outside raced on without them. Multiple towns, without the power to protect themselves, were overtaken by developers or the government—torn down or else flooded beneath man-made lakes.

The ghost towns and lost communities in this book are in varying stages of decay. Some are remarkably well preserved, allowing visitors to literally step back in time. For some, however, all that remains are ruins hidden among the trees, reclaimed by nature.

Exploring Ghost Towns Firsthand; Hearing Stories from People Who Lived There

In the making of this book, I traveled to visit many ghost towns and lost communities firsthand, taking photos that reveal how they appear today compared with archival images from their heyday. I wanted to allow readers a chance to "see" these places for themselves.

Also, I wanted to do more than simply project my own idea of history onto these lost communities, which can no longer speak for themselves. I did my best to find people with deep roots or to collect oral histories so the voices of these places could be heard louder than my own.

Finally, I tried to choose locations that allow visitors to come explore. So I hope this will be more than just a history book but, rather, a starting point for your own adventure.

Keeping History Alive, Even After It's Gone

Ever since I was a five-year-old girl, scrawling stories with hand-drawn artwork in tattered notebooks, one of my biggest dreams in life has always been to publish my own book.

As I got older, I found I loved telling stories that were most at risk of being forgotten. I loved listening to the elder generation tell me about times past—both good and bad—and ensuring those memories had a place of honor in the stories I wrote. As a seventh-generation North Carolinian who has watched my own history be torn down firsthand, it became even more important to make sure these places are remembered.

So this book is truly the culmination, not just of my personal dream, but of a grander dream: that the stories of lost communities not be forgotten.

Chapter 1

MERRY OAKS

Decay and Demolition Threaten Lost Town

Hidden down a rural side road off a main highway in Chatham County is an abandoned 1800s village whose story went viral in 2024 after it went up for sale for less than $500,000—cheaper than the cost of a single house in Raleigh. For roughly a year, the surrounding community held its breath, silently praying that whoever finally bought it would choose to save it, restore it, and not demolish it.

Today, it looks like a ghost town. It's nearly all that remains of the once thriving railroad community of Merry Oaks.

The abandoned stretch of village, which once served as the main street of Merry Oaks, runs parallel along the Seaboard Air Line railroad tracks that the community was built around. It includes three major buildings: a grand old railroad hotel, a little post office, and an old-timey general store. Some say that, once upon a time, a little railroad depot also stood on the land, but it has since decayed and fallen apart. Merry Oaks was also an educational center for Chatham County, boasting the county's first public school in 1908.

According to local legend, the land around Merry Oaks has inspired joy, music, and dance for hundreds of years. A 1951 article in the *Chatham Record* attributed the name to the Indigenous tribes who lived on the land for generations before European settlers arrived, saying the enchanting ring of towering oaks was a favorite spot for making campfires, cooking their food, and dancing beneath the branches. They called this magical spot the "Merry Oaks."

The former Merry Oaks Post Office has been abandoned and now sits alongside the vacant railroad hotel and general store. *Author's personal collection.*

When European merchants and farmers began moving into the area around 1870, they also began to gather in the center of town for evenings of music beneath the trees.

Sadly, despite having roots in joy and merriment, the story of Merry Oaks is a cautionary tale of how entire communities are lost. The hearty railroad village survived multiple wars and the 1918 Spanish flu outbreak—but it was no match for the ever-changing world of development and industrialization. Larger towns grew nearby, luring residents away with the promise of better job opportunities and schools. Widening highways and new developments destroyed historic homes and churches. Eventually, in the wake of World War II, the town was stripped of its incorporation status and wiped off the map.

It's a fight the handful of remaining residents are still fighting—the same fight, just a new time period. In recent years, some of the town's last remaining historic structures have faced demolition. In the summer of 2025, after years of pushing for preservation, the heartbroken community gathered to watch bulldozers destroy their beautiful Merry Oaks Baptist Church, which had watched over the town from its grassy field for nearly 140 years.

For many months, the fate of their historic railroad house, general store, and post office sat on the edge of a coin flip. Would the new owners demolish the heart of the community—or restore it so future generations could once again gather and dance in the center of town?

You can imagine the relief when, mere months after the church was destroyed, the announcement came: that historic stretch of Merry Oaks had been purchased, and it would become a gathering place once again.

Frozen in Time: Abandoned Village Is a Time Capsule from 1800s

Like many communities settled in the late 1800s, the main stretch of Merry Oaks was built along a railroad route.

Merry Oaks was once a thriving square-mile railroad town with multiple general stores, farms, and mills that made good money shipping lumber and other products to the nearby capital city of Raleigh. A magnificent railroad

Frozen in time: The main stretch of Merry Oaks has been sitting vacant for years. Today, it's overgrown, and current owners are working on repairs. *Author's personal collection.*

hotel, standing between the general store and the post office, saw bustling activity as the trains rumbled past, picking up shipments, collecting mailbags, and dropping off travelers.

Today, the hotel, general store, and post office stand like a time capsule of the village's lost history.

EDWARDS HOTEL: EXPLORING A VACANT RAILROAD HOUSE

A grandiose yellow house in the heart of the village catches your eye immediately. In its heyday, the large wraparound porch served as the town's center stage, where Merry Oaks farmers would gather on a hot summer evening for endless jam sessions—work boots drumming on the hardwood, fingers plucking banjos and guitars, while kids danced and spun in the wide, grassy yard.

According to town legend, these joyous jam sessions were often paired with plenty of liquor. Eventually, the men would start to bet on whose horse was fastest, and they'd take off on a drunken race around the circle of towering oak trees that surrounded the property. For years, the railroad house hosted a lively variety of travelers and musicians. Today, the old hotel's seven bedrooms sit abandoned.

In recent years, the hotel was owned by a rotation of artists and storytellers who tried their best to keep its soul alive by hosting music gatherings on the front porch. Inside, a strange collection of animal skulls and lost hubcaps decorates the peeling walls. One bedroom is adorned with a charcoal rubbing of an eerie 1700s gravestone. On the front porch, old wooden rocking chairs invite visitors to sit—just like the farmers used to do. Up above, a balcony provides a breathtaking view of the entire yard.

The home was originally built as a one-story house with two rooms. Around 1890, it was expanded into the impressive two-story house and hotel you see today. Old newspapers advertise the home as the Edwards Hotel. Around the turn of the century, it was owned by William Turner Edwards, a prominent local who arrived in Merry Oaks in the late 1800s with dreams of becoming a successful merchant. He served as the town's postmaster and mayor, and he was a major supporter in the push for establishing the high school.

Eventually, the hotel was passed to one of Mr. and Mrs. Edwardses' nieces, a woman named Grace Truett, who lived there in 1915 while teaching at the nearby Merry Oaks School. By 1972, a woman named Ann Hill had

A modern-day look at the former Edwards Hotel. Built in the 1800s, the railroad hotel was central to the town's growth. *Author's personal collection.*

purchased all four structures along the railroad tracks. She is remembered fondly by residents even today, and her unique art and quirky personality are still visible in the decor across the village.

Despite its age and vacancy, the old hotel is in relatively good condition, with strong wooden floors and a creaky staircase leading to sunlit bedrooms with large windows. One glimpse out these windows reveals a sight that hasn't changed in more than a century—the old Yates & Thomas General Store, propped up on a stone foundation, looking exactly like a flashback from the 1800s.

The Yates & Thomas General Store: From Bustling Village Center to Quiet Tenant House

A beautiful side yard creates a grassy alleyway between the railroad house and the general store. Fallen wooden gates and decaying fences divide the

An archival photo of the old Yates & Thomas General Store in its prime. *Courtesy of the Chatham County Historical Association.*

A modern-day look at the former Yates & Thomas General Store. *Author's personal collection.*

yard, and a covered brick well sits conveniently between the two structures. You can almost imagine chickens running around the yard, while kids weave jump ropes out of vines and chant nursery rhymes. Nearby, an abandoned chicken coop adds to the ambience.

A photo from 1893 shows the Yates & Thomas General Store in its prime. The two-story gable-front frame store features a combination of Victorian and Italianate architecture styles, with sheathed German siding, a hip-roof porch, and two brick chimney stacks. It features a three-bay façade and double-leaf doors. Back then, a fine set of stairs right in front of the building led up to the wooden porch and double doors. Today, those stairs are gone, leaving a gaping view of the porch's dark underside, standing on a few pillars of stone.

Like the railroad house, the general store has a balcony overhead, complete with another set of double doors. In those days, it was common for a family to live in the upstairs of their own store.

The backyard view of the store is particularly impressive. It almost looks like a ski lodge, with dark brown wooden siding and colorful red and teal doors. Inside, you can almost envision where the store's shelves once attached to the walls, where rows of products once waited to be bought. Wooden rafters are visible along the ceiling, and the former kitchen was more recently used for storing artwork.

The bustling old store—full of community chatter, travelers, and gossip—was eventually transformed into a quiet tenant house.

A Good Childhood: Growing Up in Merry Oaks

In its heyday in the early 1900s, Merry Oaks was a burgeoning town, featuring the railroad hotel, multiple general stores, a bank, a blacksmith, a train depot, a shoe shop, a feed and farm store, and a boarding school. One by one, these places began to close shop and fade from the landscape.

When Kay Hinsley drives through the square mile that once made up the town of Merry Oaks, she can still see the ghosts of the places that made up her childhood home. Her roots grow as deep as the oaks themselves.

"I'm one of the last few people born and raised in Merry Oaks who still lives here," said Hinsley.

CHILDHOOD IN A GENERAL STORE

For the first five years of her life, Hinsley grew up in a general store owned by her family. Then she moved into the former Merry Oaks Academy, which had been bought by her grandparents after the school closed down.

She recalls the family store was named Lisk, after her uncle. Eventually, it became Bud's Place and then Howard's Place. "It passed through the family for quite a few generations," she said. "The name would change when it passed to a new family member."

From 1953 until 1958, she lived in the store—and the community was her family.

"In the back of the store there was a raised area where they kept all the feed for the animals," she recalled. "Well, they hauled away the feed and turned that space into a little apartment for my family. A little kitchen and a

Norton Lisk, father to Johnny Lisk, standing at the counter of the family general store. To Kay, he was known as Uncle Norton. *Courtesy of Kay Hinsley.*

living room. That's when my mama and daddy owned it, and the sign would have said 'Howards.'"

Not many kids can say their childhood home was full of glass candy dispensers, old Coca-Cola chests, loose tobacco, and cigarettes. But growing up in a general store, Hinsley remembers all the aisles in her home—full of lotions, soaps, shoes, work clothes, and feed sacks.

"The men folk had a card table over with the feed sacks," she said. "They'd play Rook and run their mouths. I was always upset because I wasn't allowed to go over there as a kid."

She laughed. "They probably thought I'd hear a bad word."

Most of all, she recalled, the store was a gathering place for the community—and it gave her a huge sense of family.

"Always people in the store, coming in and out. They became family," she recalled. "I had several uncles and daddies and several aunts. None of them were related, and I loved them all."

It was a small-town feel; you knew everybody.

"You had the characters in the community," she said. "And it was a walking community. I could go get eggs from a neighbor. Then I'd go over someplace and get my butter. We knew all the people to see to get what we needed."

Moving into the Old Merry Oaks Academy Schoolhouse

When Hinsley's grandmother passed away in 1958, her family moved out of the family store and into the former Merry Oaks Academy, which had been the first public school in Chatham County long before Merry Oaks was unincorporated. It had opened to much fanfare in 1908, serving as both a local and boarding school for twenty to thirty students. Hinsley's grandparents B.G. Windham and Pearl Womack Windham purchased the schoolhouse from the Chatham Board of Education in 1930 and began renovations to turn it into a family home.

"They turned the first floor into living quarters and put up some walls so we had a kitchen, dining room, living room, bathroom, and foyer," said Hinsley. "And we had what we called the 'front room.' When we got older, we could have our boyfriends come visit us there."

A treasure-trove of old schoolbooks was hidden in the attic, but Hinsley jokes they were guarded by bats. "If I got the nerve as a kid, I'd go in there to look at those old books. But I had to be worried about the bats," she laughed.

Merry Oaks High School, the first public school in Chatham County. Sisters Kay Hinsley and Sharon Baker would later grow up here. *Courtesy of the Chatham County Historical Association.*

Hinsley said there weren't a lot of other kids around her age in the area, but she was the middle child with two other sisters. She spent her time outdoors playing ball, getting on the swing set, and pulling mudbugs out of the pond. "I was one of these tomboy kids that would grab a lizard and throw it at my sister," she smiled. "I would terrorize her."

Her grandparents' house was right behind the family store, and her great-grandmother lived in another house nearby. "We all lived right there together for a while," she said.

Sadly, the historic schoolhouse—and Hinsley's childhood home—was destroyed. "Lightning struck the house in 1970," she recalled. "Our neighbor actually saw the lightning strike a tree and a fireball roll off the tree and onto the house."

At the time, Hinsley was living in Cary. She broke land speed records racing to her old home.

"It burned to the ground in maybe two hours," she said. "We just stood there and cried. That was my childhood home."

Evelyn (Windham) Howard sitting on the steps outside her mother's home, the former Merry Oaks High School. Courtesy of Sharon Baker.

Hinsley eventually built a new house on the same piece of land. "So I still live on my old homeplace," she said.

And from that house on her family land, she watches as the remains of Merry Oaks are torn down all around her.

Bulldozed Our History

Until recently, Hinsley had been watching a highway widening project that threatened to take away one of the few remaining pillars of her hometown's history: the Merry Oaks Baptist Church.

The church was demolished, despite many efforts to save it. Still reeling from that loss, she says recent plans from the North Carolina Department of Transportation could displace twenty-seven homes and five businesses. The highway is expanding to accommodate potential traffic increases that could come along with a new automobile manufacturing plant from overseas; however, some locals aren't even sure the plant will ever be built.

"It's not the first time," said Hinsley. A highway built in 1958 split her grandmother's property in half. "A lot of people in Merry Oaks lost a lot when the US-1 bypass came through. Now with the new plant, there's more 'improvements' that'll basically wipe out Merry Oaks.

"You just bulldozed our history," she said grimly.

"A Town That Was": How History Gets Demolished

How does a thriving town get entirely wiped off the map?

Some ghost towns are destroyed by floods or fires. One ghost town we explore in this book was destroyed in a war. Merry Oaks is being destroyed by industrialization and developers. In the pursuit of progress, the slow-paced and simple lifestyle was left behind. Nearby, some contemporary towns flourished as they adapted to the new world. Meanwhile, Merry Oaks has been slowly fading—losing its history bit by bit until almost nothing remains.

Merry Oaks originally began thriving because it was sitting on the cutting edge of technology: lumber mills and a railroad. The trains grumbled through town each day, shipping off valuable Merry Oaks lumber directly to the capital city and carrying travelers to the Edwards Hotel.

But lumber and gristmills fell by the wayside as electricity took over more households. Likewise, as automobiles grew in accessibility, the popularity of railroads began to decline.

After this hit to its job economy, Merry Oaks took another major blow, this time to its education system, when Merry Oaks Academy closed in 1921. A newer school in Moncure drew students away, lowering enrollment. At the same time, younger generations who didn't want to farm left town to seek their fortune in places like Moncure or Pittsboro.

The exodus put a strain on the bank and stores, which began closing in the 1920s. Travelers began using their own cars instead of the train, putting a strain on the hotel.

"As the leading citizens drifted away, the town soon became inactive in civic affairs," shared Barbara Wallace, who wrote a series on the history of Merry Oaks in the 1970s. "Soon there was no mayor, no magistrate, no policeman."

The Great Depression and World War II also took their toll on the rural town. By the 1950s, Merry Oaks had lost its post office and was stripped of its status as an incorporated town, essentially wiping it off the map altogether.

As soon as a decade later, the *News & Observer* wrote a 1966 article about Merry Oaks in the past tense, saying it was "once a merry little town" and describing it as full of abandoned buildings and unrecognizable ruins.

By the time Hinsley was born, Merry Oaks was no longer an official town—but there was still so much more to lose. Highways and developers destroyed what was left, and as each generation moved away, they'd take the history along with them. Now, very few people remain who can even tell the story of Merry Oaks.

That makes the few remaining historic buildings—including the stretch of village and the old church—all the more important. They are the only tangible remnants of a town whose history is being lost day by day.

"It's disappearing every day," said Hinsley sadly.

Merry Oaks Baptist Church: Losing Another Landmark

History recently repeated itself in Merry Oaks—and residents watched in anguish once again as new developments demolished one of the few remaining pieces of their community's past.

The historic Merry Oaks Baptist Church, torn down in 2025 to widen a highway. *Courtesy of Karley Michelle.*

The church was a reflection of the surrounding community: simple but beautiful. Built in 1888, it had been watching over the community for generations. A small white frame church with a gable front and simple steeple, it looked like a painting on the grassy highway corner surrounded by rustic trees and a white picket fence.

Bright red pews once held the memories of Merry Oaks itself—church potlucks, tearful weddings, Sunday school lessons, and children dressed in their Easter finest.

"Although the church is the people, it's still hard not to mourn a building. This building. The memories of our families who attended for generations. The memories of services, weddings and funerals. The beautiful hymns that still echo in our thoughts and hearts," said a social media page dedicated to memories of the church.

"We grew up in the church," recalled Hinsley, whose grandmother also attended.

Was it here in these pews that families prayed during the 1918 Spanish flu, when the nearest doctor lived all the way across the Haw River?

Many church members have questioned why the state would demolish a church with 140 years of history. Many fought to save the building—and many are now concerned how the demolition will scatter their congregation, sending memories of Merry Oaks to the wind.

One church member named Karley Michelle wrote an emotional poem in tribute to Merry Oaks Baptist. It is printed here with her permission and blessing:

"That Little White Church"

Do you remember that old white church?
The one with a steeple standing tall, at a crossroads in that little town of Merry Oaks?
That old little white church isn't the same as it once was. Once the light shined through those stained glass windows, the pews full of saints and sinners. Laughter and praise filled its sanctuary as preaching was bellowed along its walls.
No, now it sits, vacant. Empty and worn.
Just waiting for its demise in the final days to come…
No people.
No pews.
No hymns sang.
No bell rang.

It's seen its last door open.
It's heard its last sermon.
It's carried its last burden.
It's altar's seen its last tear from a sinner's eyes shed.
For "progress," so they call it, has come. It says there's no need for that old white church anymore. New roads, new beginnings is what some people seem to feel it needs.
Some newcomers may say, "What do you need that little old white church for?"
Its people have moved on, feeling no need to continue.
So this old white church becomes a memory in our minds of our forgotten South.
Our history in this small town is quickly becoming a memory and it absolutely shatters my heart.
Sometimes I feel as though we want "growth," but at what expense?
No one will ever truly know this small town of Merry Oaks like the people who live here now, in the years to come.

A New Generation: Plans to Save the Historic Stretch of Merry Oaks

Hinsley said, especially with the church being demolished, she had been praying the old hotel, general store, and post office would be saved and restored—but she didn't hold out much hope.

Not far away, several similar rural communities lost their own battles with eminent domain and now sit on the bottom of Jordan Lake. One such community, named Seaforth, was washed away completely.

"Both sides of my family have lost their homes to 'progress.' My mom's was Merry Oaks. My dad's was Seaforth. So many of those little communities—no one even knows their names anymore," Hinsley said.

But despite it all, she'd live it all over again.

"I loved growing up here. It was really simple and beautiful," she said. "And no matter how much it changes, it'll always be Merry Oaks."

Fortunately, in the final hour, two families stepped forward to take on the task of reviving Merry Oaks. They've purchased the tract of land with the railroad hotel, post office, and general store. Now, they are faced with the challenge of rescuing the aging structures and reviving the spirit of a beloved community gathering space.

Two couples—Andrea and Dave Harling and Malia and Jerry Paul—bought the property with a dream of creating a giant Halloween Haunt. Once they began touring the property, hearing the incredible stories and rich history, they realized they had something even more special than they'd originally planned.

Andrea and Malia were especially moved by tales of the town's sense of community. They learned the grand wooden front porch once hosted musicians and storytellers. They learned of the incredible and kind artist who filled the property with her creativity and love.

"We decided we wanted to host community events, just like the property had been used for previously," said Andrea.

While they will still host a giant haunt each October, they're also envisioning holiday markets, historic tours, and any kind of event that could allow the community to continue enjoying and gathering in the heart of Merry Oaks.

But before any of those dreams can become reality, they first need to stabilize the structures, especially the beautiful yellow railroad house, which has experienced significant decay. "So, we've been calling out to the community for help," explained Andrea. "Hosting fundraisers to help pay for the initial expense of stabilizing these old, historic structures."

As the two families are introduced to Merry Oaks, they've found support from local historians who have lived in Merry Oaks for decades, as well as historic groups that have offered to help. Some locals and historians have already reached out to make sure these two families understand the immense cultural value of the land they are now in charge of protecting.

"The interest and support we've gotten so far has been really encouraging," says Andrea.

For a town that's lost so much, perhaps that sense of community is what will hold it together for generations to come.

Chapter 2

BRUNSWICK TOWN

Colonial-Era Ghost Town Destroyed in the Revolutionary War

There's a place along the North Carolina coast where you can walk through three-hundred-year-old ruins of a ghost town older than the United States itself.

The story of Brunswick Town is a bit different than some of the other ghost towns in this book. Far from a tiny rural mill village or small farming community, lost in a flood or a shift in the economy, Brunswick Town was a bustling port town full of wealthy homes—including a royal governor's castle—until it was destroyed by the rage of the Revolutionary War.

It's not shocking, however, that this colonial port town would be targeted by the British as they marched through the Carolinas. The seeds of revolution were growing here in Brunswick Town long before the famous Boston Tea Party saw colonists chanting, "No taxation without representation!" Archaeologists have even discovered artifacts with secret codes hidden in the floorboards of the town's tavern—evidence of many nights of drinking, secrecy, and sedition.

So let's explore what life was like in a port town so full of Patriots and Revolutionaries that it was eventually pummeled with cannons, buffeted by musket balls and burned down by soldiers determined to root out revolution during the birth of the United States.

Despite being blitzed with cannonballs and muskets, St. Philip's Church is the most complete aboveground structure in Brunswick Town. *Author's personal collection.*

Seeds of Revolution Still Visible Three Hundred Years Later

Step into Brunswick Town today, and you can almost feel yourself transported back in time. Strolling along the waterfront of the Cape Fear, where curtains of Spanish moss wave from the branches of gnarled old trees in the salty coastal air, you can catch a glimpse of a vista that dates back more than three hundred years.

Layout of the Lost Community

It's easy to see why English colonists would choose to settle here along the bluffs overlooking the river. Like walking through a map from the 1700s, you can actually see the footprints of their homes and shops along the trail. Stone foundations standing several feet tall reveal the size and layout of the houses. Gaps in the walls show where side doors once led into basement areas, which often held storefronts, allowing families to live in the upper floors. Well-preserved brick remains of fireplaces are still visible in the old

Foundations of homes from the 1700s create a visual "map" of how Brunswick Town once appeared. *Author's personal collection.*

living quarters, conjuring images of patriotic families sitting by the fire on cold winter evenings, perhaps knitting while the kids play with wooden toys and adults worry over politics.

Some lots even show where internal walls divided the home into multiple rooms or where brick staircases led down to the side door.

One lot with multiple rooms and walls stretches far longer than the others. The lot includes six rooms, each divided by a wall. A hearth in the center of the wall served two rooms, with archaeologists discovering decorative tile around the fireplace. There appears to have been a central entrance and public yard in front of the complex. Archaeologists uncovered artifacts like glass beads; thousands of brass straight pins; buttons made of bone, copper, or silver; cufflinks; and scissors. Historians theorize this may have been a public house and tavern, where travelers and sailors could grab a drink and rent a room for the night.

Some of the homesite ruins have grass, foliage, or even small trees growing inside their walls—a somber reminder that, although we can catch glimpses back in time to this bustling 1700s port town, the community truly has become a ghost town.

The ruins of Brunswick Town regularly reveal new secrets, according to site manager, author, and historian Jim McKee. "Creating the map of Brunswick Town is like piecing together a puzzle with new pieces being found all the time," he said.

St. Philip's Church

The largest and perhaps most remarkable ruin in Brunswick Town is St. Philip's Church, with stately hollowed-out walls and towering archways where a grandiose doorway once stood. Centenarian trees surround the old church like sentinels, and soft Spanish moss dangles across the vacant, vaulted windows like curtains. Where floors of hardwood and tile once formed the shape of a cross, now you'll find only a lush green carpet of grass. Where a vaulted ceiling once held mighty trusses, you'll now find only an opening to the sky above.

As incomplete as the ruin appears, it actually provides an accurate glimpse into the 1750s in Brunswick Town.

"Most of what you see today is what Governor Arthur Dobbs saw when he first arrived and saw the church for himself because at the time, it only had walls—no roof or floors," said McKee. "When you step inside, it's 1758."

Peering through a doorway to the past in the ruins of St. Philip's Church. *Author's personal collection.*

Despite being a church, St. Philip's was not protected from the ire of war. The thick brick walls bear the scars of revolution, battered with pock marks from bullets and cannonballs.

Given its size and durability, it's no surprise it's the only remaining aboveground structure in Brunswick Town. The impressive brick walls stand twenty-four feet high and up to three feet thick. The governor designated St. Philip's as "His Majesty's Chapel" for the colony.

"If the King of England had visited North Carolina, this is where he'd have attended church," said McKee.

Construction began in 1754 but continued in fits and starts for many years. If you stand on the sidewalk today and look at the church walls, you'll count eight different color changes in either the brick or mortar. These layers represent construction "episodes," which occurred whenever a new shipment of construction equipment arrived.

"It took them two to three years to get those walls up," said McKee. "It's uniform all the way around."

By 1760, McKee said, they had managed to get a roof on the church. But shortly after, it was struck by lightning. Shortly after that, a storm struck and the roof collapsed—a harsh blow, taking down an estimated seventeen thousand shingles.

Seed money to help fund the large price tag of construction came from an odd twist of fate. In 1748, several years before construction on the church began, a ship full of Spanish privateers attacked Brunswick Town, driving many of the colonists into the surrounding woods to hide and watch helplessly as their homes were raided. However, the next day, the town's port collector, William Dry III—a Patriot whose story and deeds will continue later in this chapter—gathered sixty-seven armed men to retake the town. These men included William Moore, Schenk Moore, Edward Wingate, Cornelius Harnett Jr., and William Lord.

The remains of the ship, called *La Fortuna*, were plundered from the river, bringing immense wealth to Brunswick Town, while also giving the community a "rough and tough" reputation that prevented further attacks from privateers. Items salvaged from *La Fortuna* provided seed money for building St. Philip's Church.

Once the rooftop was secured, builders began crafting the church interior. They began with building eight brick bases along the ground and then building columns to support the roof and trusses. A broad walkway led from the main doors, creating an aisle to the altar pad. Then, a tile walkway stretched from the north to the south entrance, so that if you looked down from above, the walkways formed the shape of a big cross.

There was also a narrow tile walkway around the inside perimeter of the church, creating four blank quadrants. Wooden floors were laid down in each quad, supporting pews.

Historians believe there's a church standing today that has an identical interior to St. Philip's. St. James Episcopal Church in Santee, South Carolina, has been untouched for all these centuries.

"We think those are sister churches," said McKee.

Remains of a Royal Governor's Former Castle—and His Toilet

There's one other large ruin hidden in this colonial-era ghost town—and it's a castle!

Captain John Russel began work on his grand home in the early 1750s. The large, multistory home stood between Brunswick Town and Roger Moore's Orton Plantation.

Russel died before the home was completed, and the home sat vacant until 1758, when Royal Governor Arthur Dobbs arrived to view Brunswick Town. The town offered to sell Dobbs the home for a shilling per acre and one peppercorn.

"Peppercorn couldn't be harvested until the following year, so this guaranteed he'd stay at least a year," explained McKee. "And since at the time the colony's capital was determined by wherever the governor resided, this guaranteed Brunswick Town would be the capital for at least a year."

The ruins of North Carolina's first Governor's Mansion, known today as Russelborough. *Author's personal collection.*

At the end of the year, the townspeople waited eagerly to see if Dobbs would pay the final amount due on his residence. Sure enough, he handed over a peppercorn—and from 1758 until 1770, Brunswick Town was the capital. This helped drive the importance of the town, and the community really entered its heyday.

Once Dobbs purchased Russelborough, he changed the name to Castle Dobbs. Today, the ruins of his "castle" provide insight into what life was like inside.

There's a large outer wall of stone foundation—representing a complete wraparound porch that encompassed all four sides of the home—surrounding a smaller inner wall. Some of the internal foundation forms a grid, revealing the layout of the first-floor rooms. One room has a brick well inside, which historians believed was used to keep wine cool. Another room appears to have ruins of a fireplace. While most of the floors are gone, stamped down into the dirt, there are two small sections where some original flooring made of tile or small stones can be seen.

Perhaps one of the most interesting features is the tunnel in the northeast corner of the home's foundation. "There were a lot of theories over what that tunnel was," grins McKee. "It's actually the sewer. Russelborough has the oldest flush toilet found in North Carolina."

When the colonial-era toilet was discovered in 1964, it was taken to Raleigh for research. There, it remained for decades until 2017, when McKee pushed to have the historic toilet returned to Brunswick Town to be used in an exhibit.

The toilet's roots apparently trace back to Ireland, where Irish historians had also found a similar colonial-era toilet and were trying to solve the same mystery as North Carolina's historians—what is the story behind this unusual toilet?

"In 2019, I got an email from an archaeologist in Ireland, and they had found a toilet just like ours in Ireland. It had been in a cemetery for 100+ years, being used as a planter. They were online looking for photos of colonial toilets, and ours popped up!" said McKee. "They are exactly the same, except theirs is made of limestone and ours is made of coquina."

A paper trail showed the Irish toilet had originated in a nearby building that, centuries prior, had been the last place Dobbs lived before coming to North Carolina. It seems likely, then, that Dobbs brought the technology of flushing toilets with him from Ireland to Brunswick Town. This wouldn't be shocking, given Dobbs's talent as an architect. He designed and built Ireland's parliament building. One of North Carolina's most accomplished governors, he was

North Carolina's first toilet? This unusual tunnel in the foundation of Russelborough is an example of early indoor plumbing. *Author's personal collection.*

also an explorer with an interest in the Northwest Passage, an entomologist who wrote extensively on the American honeybee, an astronomer who wrote heavily on the appearance of "Sun Dogs," and a biologist who discovered the Venus flytrap right here along the Carolina coast.

Dobbs can also be thanked for providing over 400,000 acres of North Carolina real estate for Irish settlers. While the Irish didn't ultimately take him up on the offer, the Highland Scots did – and the region still has historic ties to the Highlands to this day.

Later, when Governor William Tryon bought Russelborough, he changed the name to Castle Tryon. He wrote a letter in 1765 that described the grand home:

> *This house which has so many assistances is of an oblong square, built of wood. It measured on the outside faces forty five feet by thirty five feet and is divided into two Stories exclusive of the Cellars; the parlour is about five feet above the surface of the Earth. Each Story has four Rooms and three light Closets. The Parlour below and Drawing Room are 20 x 15*

Today, Brunswick Town's ruins have trees and plants growing inside. *Author's personal collection.*

> *feet each: Ceilings low. There is a Piazza runs around the House both stories of ten feet wide with a Balustrade of four feet high, which is a great security for my little Girl. There is a good Stable and Coach Houses, and some other Out Houses.*

The ruins of the Tryon-era kitchen are partially excavated on the north side of the mansion.

Today, if you stand outside Russelborough's ruins and look out at the marsh, you'll see the spot where fields of rice once grew around the plantation. Directly across the river, you can see Snow's Cut Bridge, which takes you across to Carolina Beach.

Day-to-Day Life in Brunswick Town

Founded in 1726 by Maurice Moore, Brunswick Town grew into a bustling port town, exporting tar, pitch, and turpentine, which were derived from

North Carolina's expansive natural resource of longleaf pine. Used for building and maintaining the Royal Navy and merchant ships, these exports helped Brunswick Town flourish.

At its peak in the 1760s, Brunswick Town had around 250 colonists—smaller than Wilmington, which had closer to 800.

Brunswick's wealth and influence, brought on partially by its valuable exports and partially by having two consecutive royal governors as residents, made it a desirable and attractive place to live.

"I joke that Brunswick is the first gated community," laughed McKee. "It had an HOA, basically. When you purchased a piece of property, you had a certain amount of time to do something with it—develop it, rent it, resell it. If you were going to develop it, you had minimum standards you had to build to. And if your house or building was damaged or destroyed, you had a certain amount of time to effect repairs or tear it down and rebuild it."

One homesite ruin provides a perfect example of this mentality.

"When the McCorckle house burned down in 1773 or 1774, they tore it down and never rebuilt it. When the archaeologist went to excavate it, they found no artifacts at all. Just beach sand and debris. Looks like after the house burned, they back-filled the house with debris and covered it with sand. Ready for resell," said McKee.

A Beach-House Community with an Enslaved Population

McKee said if you could afford property in Brunswick, odds were high you also had property elsewhere—meaning Brunswick Town was essentially a "beach-house" community made up of second homes. "Many families had maybe a plantation or a house in Wilmington," said McKee. "This was a second house."

McKee said that in the summertime when the heat is fierce, the humidity is strong, and the alligators are active in the nearby marsh, many families would leave Brunswick and go to their main homes in more favorable climates.

"But you couldn't just leave your house with no one to keep it up, so…" he said. "During the summer months, the men and women enslaved by these families would live in the houses and maintain them."

"They would live in the half-cellar downstairs. Or sometimes in the outdoor summer kitchen."

If the homeowner was a merchant, the half-cellar usually had a street-level entrance, and customers would enter beneath the porch. During the summer, it was likely enslaved men and women would also manage the shops.

A labor force of enslaved families also worked in the shipyards, harvesting rice from the nearby plantations and constructing buildings around town.

The more the European colonists pushed for freedom in the form of revolution, the more pressure they began putting on the enslaved families. Brunswick Town relies on the Royal Navy purchasing their exports, so on the eve of the American Revolution, they began to expand rice cultivation. This required a massive workforce to go into the swamps, cut down trees, remove stumps, and dig canals—ballooning the demand for more enslaved men and women to work in these treacherous conditions.

In 1773, Orton Pond was created to irrigate the upland fields at nearby plantations.

When the Revolutionary War began, at least one hundred enslaved people escaped to British lines, with many rushing to join the Royal Navy for the promise of freedom. However, it's important to note that many free and enslaved Black soldiers fought on the side of the Patriots, as well. Some North Carolina cities like Halifax have done work in recent years to highlight the lost stories of these soldiers.

Secret Signet Rings and Seditious Seals: Birth of a Revolution

Taverns have always been places where real history is made quietly, out of the eyesight of historians and newspapers. During an era when politicians had to travel by horseback to the capital, taverns were dark places where they could rest for the night, toasting in hushed voices to future plans for the state.

So when McKee's team found a tavern's ruins in Brunswick Town in 2018, they were excited. They knew they'd uncovered a big ruin, but it wasn't listed on the map. Excavations confirmed tavern-related artifacts, but historians still had a lot of questions.

Then, they found a little blue jewel, about a third the size of a dime. Embossed on it was a phrase: "Wilkes and Liberty 45." "That was a slogan back then, but it didn't really become generally used on this side of the pond until after 1769–70," said McKee. "It is definitely seditious in terms of anti-government."

Archaeologists uncovered a tiny stone in the floorboards of the tavern, believed to be from a signet ring that held a secret code. *Courtesy of Brunswick Town State Historic Site.*

McKee said they believe the stone is either the insert to a cufflink or the insert on a signet ring. It had fallen between the floorboards and rested deep under the tavern for centuries.

"It's something small, something someone could discreetly show to someone else," said McKee. "It's one of the earliest symbols of sedition in North Carolina."

They also found another symbol of sedition: a William Dry bottle seal reading "W. Dry. Cape Fear. 1766."

"William Dry is the single individual who ties together the bulk of the history of Brunswick Town," explained McKee.

Dry was known to emboss personal seals on his wine bottles, but typically you'd only create a bottle seal with a specific date if you wanted to commemorate something special that had happened that year.

As it turns out, 1766 was a very big year for Brunswick Town—and for all of the future United States. That's the year the Stamp Act was repealed by British Parliament.

"My theory is Dry instigated that revolt," said McKee. "That he instigated the Stamp Act Crisis."

The Stamp Act Crisis of 1766

The seeds of revolution were born in Brunswick Town. The Stamp Act Crisis in 1766 became one of the first successful armed revolts against

British authority in America. It was a precursor to the infamous "no taxation without representation" often attributed to the Boston Tea Party.

The Stamp Act, imposed by British Parliament in 1765, forced a tax on all printed materials in the American colonies. This required colonists to affix a stamp to documents like newspapers, playing cards, pamphlets, and all other paper documents. Essentially, this put a tax on the paper itself.

In retaliation, armed residents prevented a ship called *Diligence*, which was carrying stamped paper, from unloading at their port—which was one of the most important and busy ports in the region. With no access to "legal" stamped paper, newspapers were unavailable, court could not be held, marriage licenses could not be issued—life ground to a halt.

Royal Governor Tryon felt sympathy for both sides of the issue and offered to personally pay for the stamps, but he was refused.

Judge Maurice Moore, son of the town's founder, released a pamphlet denouncing the Stamp Act called "The Justice and Policy of Taxing the American Colonies in Great Britain Considered." He wrote that the colonies could not "with the least degree of justice be taxed by British Parliament."

Things came to a head in February 1766 when two ships—the *Dobbs* and the *Patience*—were detained in Brunswick Town's port because their items were not stamped. Patriot leaders from Brunswick Town like John Ashe, Cornelius Harnett, James Moore, and Colonel Hugh Waddell led hundreds of armed citizens to surround Governor Tryon's "castle" at Russelborough.

"They surround his house and demand the two ships be released. Tryon tells them to go talk to the port collector, William Dry. The crowd left fifty or sixty men for Tryon's 'protection' and went to Dry's house," explained McKee. "Dry, who everyone knows is a Patriot, tells the crowd, 'I'm just a port collector. You need to talk to Captain Jacob Lobb on the HMS *Viper*. He's the one who actually seized the vessels.'"

The armed crowd didn't leave any guards for Dry because, despite technically working for the British government, he was such a vocal Patriot.

"When the crowd goes to the waterfront to confront Lobb, he tells them Dry is the one who ordered him to seize the ships," grinned McKee.

The angry crowd rushed back to Dry's house to confront him—but he had already vanished. And word reached them that the two ships had already been released.

"Why didn't Dry tell them, since he's the one who ordered the ships be seized? And he's also the one who released them," asked McKee. "I think he set it all up. He had to work within the legal system to stir up a revolt. So he had the two ships seized knowing it would blow everything up—and that's exactly what it does. The revolt ended the Stamp Act for the Cape Fear region."

"William Dry is proud of that. We believe that's why he put '1766' on his bottle seals," added McKee.

One might argue Brunswick Town's role in the Revolutionary War and the founding of the United States is the primary reason for its status as a ghost town today.

"You're looking at some of the founding fathers of sedition right here in Brunswick. If you want to find where the seeds of Revolution are planted, they are planted in the Stamp Act. This is when the Sons of Liberty are created. This is when you get taxation without representation. Everything that leads to the Revolution starts with the Stamp Act, right here in the tavern of Brunswick Town," said McKee.

British Destroy Brunswick Town

Ten years after hundreds of armed colonists forced the British into submission during the Stamp Act Crisis, the British had their revenge on Brunswick Town. As British troops marched through North Carolina during the Revolutionary War, they made sure dark whispers traveled to the residents of Brunswick Town: the redcoats were coming.

The people of Brunswick Town packed up and fled.

While most other colonial-era towns are still standing in North Carolina today, Brunswick Town is gone. Even Russelborough, the former royal governor's mansion, was destroyed.

Eyewitness accounts from as late as 1777 say the town is still here, just abandoned. "We're thinking the southern half of town is burned in 1781," said McKee. "Soldiers from the 82nd were occupying Wilmington and Brunswick."

McKee says they aren't even certain if the British fully destroyed the town. It could have been something as simple as a lightning strike in the deserted town.

Decades later, during the Civil War, Confederate soldiers came to the abandoned Brunswick Town and raided all the empty houses for supplies, perhaps dismantling anything that remained of the ghost town. They used the empty town as a base of operations and built an earthen fort around the area, calling it Fort Anderson.

For being one of the oldest known ghost towns in North Carolina, Brunswick Town still has plenty of ruins to see. Today, the remains of Brunswick Town and Fort Anderson are still there, waiting for guests to explore and hear stories from the colonists who lived here more than three hundred years ago.

Chapter 3

SOUL CITY

Ruins of a Multiracial Utopia Hidden in Warren County

While most college students in their early twenties are still figuring out what to do with their lives, Floyd McKissick Jr. was already building a city. Before he even turned thirty, the dream was gone—strangled by a struggling economy, trudging bureaucracy, and, perhaps most of all, fear and racism.

Soul City was built on a grand idea: a multiracial utopia where families of all races could live together in a thriving community and marginalized communities could find themselves with an equal slice of the economic pie.

In the hopeful afterglow of the civil rights movement, McKissick and his father—who was a well-known civil rights leader—believed in uplifting Black entrepreneurs and Black-owned businesses, helping them grow in the heart of a rural, mostly impoverished county.

"There was a greater sense of awareness dealing with equity and inclusion. A heightened level of awareness of people wanting to encourage Black entrepreneurship," said McKissick. "The president was also talking about it. Soul City fit right into these ideas. People were interested in being a part of it."

A brochure for Soul City explained the lofty idea: "Imagine a city without prejudice. A city without poverty. A brand new shining city."

Although McKissick's father made it clear that Soul City was meant to be a melting pot for all backgrounds, not to succeed as an "all-Black town," newspaper articles from the 1960s and '70s show many white residents in Warren County were terrified by the idea of Black capitalism being built in their backyards.

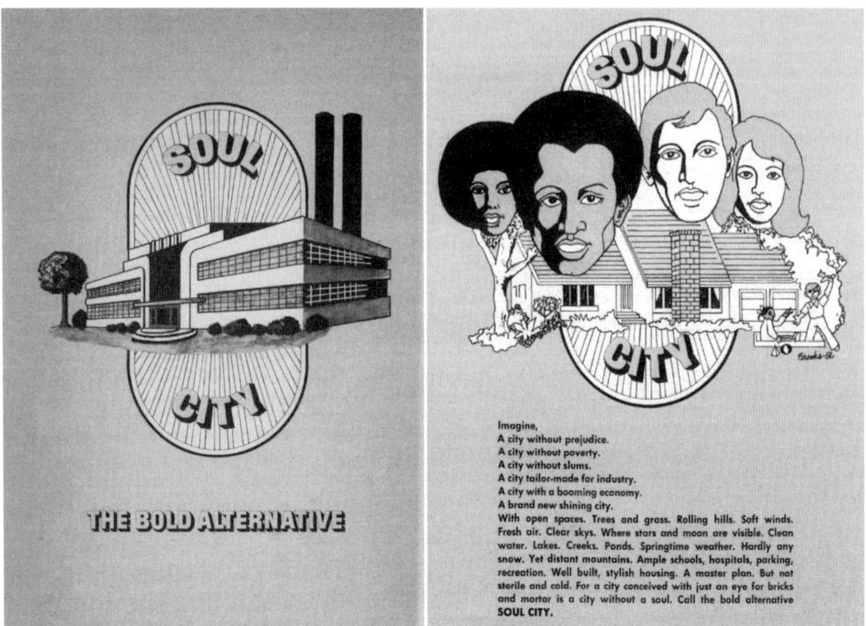

Early marketing brochure for Soul City. *Courtesy of the National Museum of African American History and Culture.*

Despite facing anxiety from some neighbors, Soul City broke ground in 1973 to much fanfare, including a parade and a speech by Governor James Holshouser, and began to grow toward its goal. McKissick planned for Soul City to encompass 3,600 acres, including affordable homes, a major industrial park, a state-of-the-art facility called Soultech 1, a healthcare facility, and Warren County's only public swimming pool.

Today, it's a safe bet to say most people in North Carolina have never heard of Soul City. Many have no idea that, as they drive up US-1 toward Virginia, they're passing the remains of this once grand dream.

Let's Explore the Remaining Pieces of Soul City

All of the guts of Soul City are still standing today. If you pull off the highway and head into town, you can see what remains from nearly half a century ago. With abandoned buildings, cracked windows, and fallen street signs, it could be easily mistaken for a ghost town. However, a small handful of people do still live in the surrounding area.

HealthCo.: Overgrown and Vacant Doctor and Dental Offices

With an old sign sitting out front, the old HealthCo. Medical and Dental building is still recognizable today. Lines of grass create green veins through broken concrete in the parking lot; broken windows surround the healthcare clinic like chipped teeth. Vandals have clearly broken inside and left their mark.

Curtains of ivy have begun hiding portions of the vacant buildings. A peek through the windows reveals a number of eerie sights: an old dental chair sitting at an odd angle in an otherwise empty room, overturned couches lying in deserted hallways, bare medical beds, and scattered supplies on the shelves.

There was a time when, according to McKissick, HealthCo. was hope on the horizon for impoverished families in Warren County. "We'd brought in doctors and dentists, and there was a van service going to pick people up," recalled McKissick. "People were living in homes covered with tar paper with no central heating, just a potbelly stove inside, and no running water."

It was the 1960s, when electricity and indoor plumbing should have been available widely, but the poverty made it seem more like the early 1900s.

Soul City aimed to bring high-quality, affordable healthcare to the surrounding area. Today, the HealthCo. building is abandoned—with old beds and dental equipment still inside. *Author's personal collection.*

"Before this, you'd have to go see a doctor another county over. You didn't make an appointment; you'd just go there and take a number. People didn't have preventative dental care or prenatal care," said McKissick. "This was transformative for people in three surrounding counties!"

Soultech I: Futuristic Employment Park Becomes Correctional Enterprise

One of the primary goals of Soul City was to offer stable jobs and opportunities for economic growth in the impoverished area of Warren County. McKissick built Soultech I, a futuristic-looking industrial incubator spanning around seventy-two thousand square feet. With roughly fifty thousand feet of manufacturing space and another twenty thousand square feet in office space, Soul City moved their offices into the building. "We had companies coming to fill that space and provide jobs," said McKissick.

The old Soultech I building was contemporary, made of concrete and solar gray glass. It was meant to become part of a larger employment park.

"One structure from the old days remains in use.…Soultech I is now the Corrections Enterprise Janitorial Products Plant," wrote Thomas Healy in his book *Soul City: Race, Equality and the Lost Dream of an American Utopia*.

"The irony is not hard to grasp," he wrote. The building, once meant to "promote Black economic freedom," has become a corrections facility "staffed by inmates earning about fifteen cents an hour."

Soultech I was an industrial incubator meant to provide quality jobs to people of Warren County. *Courtesy of the Soul City prospectus.*

Once a sign of hope coming to the region, the old wooden street signs have long since fallen down and begun to decay. *Author's personal collection.*

Freedom Circle and Liberation Road: Decaying Road Signs Point the Way

As you enter Soul City, you'll notice the street names become very poignant. Road names like Freedom Circle and Liberation Road hint at the dream that was Soul City.

Today, if you look at the ground around the green modern-day street signs, you may find the fallen, decaying wooden signs that once marked the small neighborhoods.

The Green Duke House

Sitting among the fresh new 1970s homes and civil rights-minded idealism of Soul City is an unexpected sight: a 1700s plantation house where Black men, women, and children were enslaved prior to the Civil War.

The Green Duke House stands in the center of a neighborhood, right behind the main entryway into Soul City. The Georgian-style plantation house is one of the few of its kind remaining in North Carolina. Owned by one of the earliest European families to settle in Warren County, it originally belonged to Green Duke from 1784 until 1811. His father had acquired more than three thousand acres of land in the area, according to the registration form for the National Register of Historic Places.

William Duke Jr., his father, had five daughters and only one son, Green, who inherited all of his father's land. Tax documents show Green was the owner of 4,867 acres of land—and that he enslaved thirty-five people.

The historic home was used as a daycare center for some time. It was eventually repurposed as a community center. As of 2025, a sign on the front yard designates the structure as a National Park Service project to create a McKissick Soul City Civil Rights Center.

Recreation Facilities Quietly Waiting for Families

Officially dedicated in 1977, the grassy park, quiet basketball courts, and empty swimming pool sat quietly for years, as if waiting for the hundreds of families and children who never arrived. "We had built those recreational facilities," said McKissick. "They were the only ones open to the public in a two- or three-county area."

McKissick had dreamed of children of all races and backgrounds coming from all around to enjoy playing together. "We had a pool where anybody could come to. Where Black kids could come play in a safe and attractive community," he recalled wistfully.

The Magnolia Ernest Recreation Park seems to have had a boost in recent years. After it was taken over by Warren County Parks and Recreation, a sizable grant allowed for renovations to the basketball and tennis courts, as well as upgrades to the park itself in 2022. A second phase is expected to provide more renovations to the picnic shelter and bathhouse. The pool has also been upgraded.

At a ceremony celebrating the new updates, community leaders praised McKissick's vision and said they hoped the refurbished park was "a beginning." Perhaps a small piece of McKissick's dream could come true here, and the park could be filled with the laughter and families he'd dreamed of so many decades ago.

The Soul City Sign

Like a pillar of hope that has remained standing across the generations, the original Soul City sign still welcomes visitors to explore the community that was McKissick's dream. The iconic sign has stood as a symbol for decades. One photo from the 1970s shows a multiracial group of people posing in front of the sign. Another shows McKissick's father standing and pointing into the distance.

The original Soul City sign still proudly stands, overlooking the community that could have been a multiracial utopia. *Author's personal collection.*

Even today, you can stand in front of the Soul City sign, look around at the surrounding neighborhood, and catch a feeling in the air. It's a feeling of the bittersweet challenges and triumphs of the civil rights movement. It's a feeling of change on the horizon. It's a feeling of the injustice that brought this city down.

It's a feeling of what could have been.

And, if you listen to McKissick today, maybe it's a little bit of a feeling of what still could be.

"Transforming a Region": The Beginning of Soul City

You can't discuss the origins of Soul City without first understanding McKissick and his father's roots in the civil rights movement decades beforehand. Photos and history write-ups show the senior McKissick working alongside leaders like Dr. Martin Luther King Jr. and Malcom X.

Long before the creation of Soul City, McKissick's father was a lawyer and a leader in the civil rights movement. Following his father's lead, McKissick was also active in the fight for equality, even as a child. "I was among those kids who desegregated public schools," he recalled. "I was in sixth grade. My two older sisters were pioneers in 1959 in desegregating public schools in Durham—a suit called *McKissick v. Durham City Board of Education.*"

He remembers civil rights activists gathering in his home, planning protests and sit-ins.

In the sweltering days of June 1957, a young McKissick took part in the famous pickets and sit-ins at Royal Ice Cream in Durham. "It was in a territory between a Black neighborhood and a white one. Very popular place," he said. "Black people could only get food to-go out the side entrance."

Little did he know, his sixth-grade teacher's brother was one of the shop's owners. "So obviously my teacher didn't treat me so well."

This kind of poor treatment wasn't unusual for McKissick, however. Because of his family's active work in the fight for equality, he grew up with a constant threat hanging over his head—and armed guards on his front porch to help protect them.

"We had threats all the time. That was just the norm," he said. "People would drive by and throw flyers out saying, 'You've been visited by the Knights of the KKK' to intimidate us."

Childhood trips to New York City made a major impression on McKissick, who said up north he saw a world where people were treated equally. He wanted to bring that experience down to North Carolina.

BLACK CAPITALISM: SOUL CITY AIMS TO USHER IN A NEW ERA OF EQUALITY

It all started when his father first announced Soul City and began conceptualizing what it would take to build it.

A loan from Chase Manhattan Bank got them around 1,800 acres for their first tract of land. McKissick got a degree in city and regional planning and became responsible for planning Soul City—essentially building a city from scratch while still in college. "It was fall of 1975, and I was in my last semester of grad school at UNC," he said.

McKissick's detail-oriented mind helped him stay on track—laying out roads, subdivisions, infrastructure, water and sewer, underground electric, and more. "You had to know every single little detail," he said. "How many inches of pavement? What's the cost of underground power lines? What type of streetlights? Metal poles? Posts? Do we need a lift station to pump the sewage or will we use gravity flow?"

During his entire time in grad school, he was doing the work of building Soul City alongside graduate-level studies. "The level of responsibility I had at a very young age. We're talking about $4 million a year that I'm dealing with in terms of ongoing and planned projects," he said. "I took it seriously."

For decades, the surrounding county had been struggling economically, with a large percentage of people leaving altogether. With an economy that depended on wealthy plantations, Warren County had been prosperous

A map of the original Soul City on the cover of a souvenir booklet presented at the groundbreaking. *Courtesy of Soul City.*

prior to the Civil War; however, the highly agricultural economy did not recover after losing enslaved labor. A high population of newly freed Black families put down roots in nearby communities.

By the 1970s, Warren County had one of the highest rates of residents leaving, many hoping to find opportunities elsewhere.

"Usually when they left the South and landed somewhere else, many of these families would find there was a misalignment in their skill set, and they ended up living in urban ghettos," said McKissick. "Their dreams didn't come true."

McKissick hoped Soul City would create jobs, nice homes, parks, healthcare, and educational opportunities right there in their backyards. "We wanted to provide jobs and quality of life in the place where all these people had come from to start with," he said. "They didn't have to go to Harlem; they could stay in Warren County."

While Soul City aimed to provide opportunities for all races in Warren County, they also believed in the power of Black capitalism. They wanted to build a place where Black entrepreneurs could thrive and Black voices could be part of the community leadership.

McKissick said, "Soul City was designed to provide an opportunity for African Americans to have a sense of pride and community that they could live in. They could be part of the development team. They could be decision makers, with economic and political empowerment—effectuating things my dad had talked about during the civil rights movement."

How Did We Lose Soul City?

In the same way McKissick faced personal attacks as a child in the civil rights movement, Soul City faced pushback from the surrounding community.

A 1973 article in the *News & Observer* captures the sentiment: "'What do I think about Soul City?' says one of the leathery faced men repeating the questions. 'Why I been for it all along.' He pauses and looks over at his buddies. 'I think all the [racial explicit] should move in there and we could put a fence around it and let 'em stay there.' His buddies smile big silent smiles."

Even further back, a 1969 article expresses that some of the white residents feared all of Warren County would be ruined by Soul City and that "all the white folks were going to have to leave."

"They feared a Negro takeover of political power and an influx of young hoodlums from city slums," the article continues.

McKissick says Soul City was always intended to benefit people of all races and backgrounds, especially in Warren County. It was meant to bring affordable, quality homes and healthcare, as well as jobs and education.

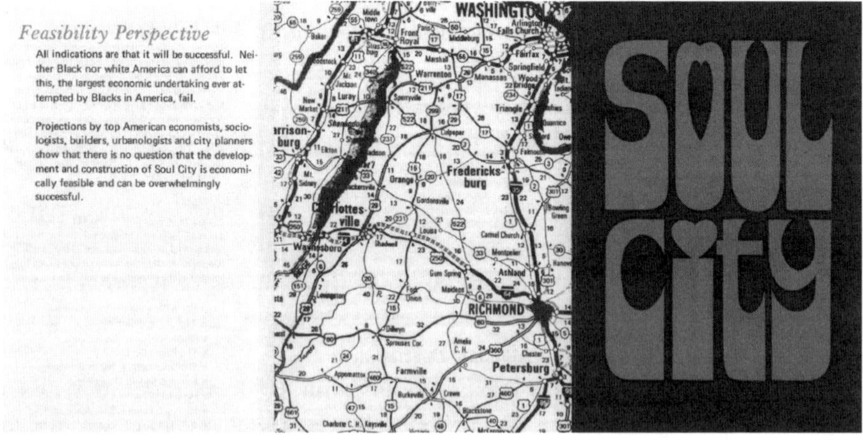

Feasibility Perspective

All indications are that it will be successful. Neither Black nor white America can afford to let this, the largest economic undertaking ever attempted by Blacks in America, fail.

Projections by top American economists, sociologists, builders, urbanologists and city planners show that there is no question that the development and construction of Soul City is economically feasible and can be overwhelmingly successful.

An informational pamphlet from the beginnings of Soul City. *Courtesy of Soul City prospectus.*

"A house around 1,400 square feet was going for about $25,000 to $30,000. People were lining up to buy these homes!" he recalled. "These homes are going to some people who struggled to get a home any other way—and they could get a nice one! Energy-efficient, low cost of utilities. Affordable mortgage."

McKissick says government officials like Senator Jesse Helms targeted the Soul City project. Likewise, a slew of *News & Observer* articles came out very critical against Soul City, despite the U.S. Department of Housing and Urban Development defending the project.

"Jesse Helms comes in and makes fraudulent allegations of fraud in our project," said McKissick. "And next thing you know the federal government is coming in and doing an audit. We got a clean bill of health—but it generated negative publicity."

Despite the audit clearing McKissick and Soul City of any wrongdoing, the damage had been done. Programs had been stalled and delayed, costing the project money and time.

"It had been seen in such a positive light before all that," said McKissick. "We had major Fortune 500 businesses looking at Soul City, and they saw all these allegations and got cold feet. They didn't want to come into a 'troubled project.'"

There were other factors that brought challenges to Soul City. Economic struggles in the United States at the time impacted construction costs, and sluggish bureaucracy cost time and money.

"The great challenge with the New Communities Administration is that they did not really understand the challenges of development. Approvals may take six months instead of six weeks—and that doesn't work. And the time is costing you money; you're spinning your wheels waiting. The whole time you're paying interest on that debt," explained McKissick.

In 1974, a new oil embargo also shot costs of oil barrels from around six dollars to around thirty-eight dollars each. "Construction costs all jumped by several hundred percent," he said.

After years of hard work, McKissick remembered the day they got the announcement that the government was withdrawing their support. "In that moment, I felt profound disappointment," he said. "Knowing a lot of the things I've worked on would probably not come to fruition."

He was only around twenty-seven years old when he watched the plug pulled on his dream.

"I mean, we all knew racism existed. We all knew how bitter it was. We all knew what we were trying to overcome," he said. "The challenging thing was to see them, in the end, being able to stop us. We weren't even given the opportunity to fail."

Roads were stopped in their tracks. Water and sewer lines halted. All projects terminated. McKissick had been planning to build an amphitheater for five thousand for a Soul City concert series that would play each year.

It would be enough to make anyone bitter—but McKissick decided to keep dreaming and keep fighting for equality for all.

Fighting for Future Generations

McKissick, a lawyer like his father, stepped into politics as a new way of building a better future.

He joined Young Democrats in Warren County and taught high schoolers how to get involved in the political process. "We were transforming the political landscape of Warren County," he smiled. "I took a busload of those kids up to Jimmy Carter's inauguration. Most of them had never left Warren County before. They got a chance to meet the governor. By the time Soul City was winding down, I had become chairman of the Democratic Party in Warren County. I was already interested in running for elected office."

He would eventually serve on the planning commission in Durham and eventually City Council. He became the chairman of the Durham County Democratic Party. In time, he was appointed by Governor Easley to fill a vacancy for senator and served six terms in the state senate.

"When I was in school, they didn't think an African American child could learn anything. The best you could hope was to excel in sports," he said.

No one in his school would have believed he'd grow up to get graduate degrees from Harvard, Duke and UNC; become a lawyer in the nation's capital; and serve in the state senate or city council.

"That's why you stand up and fight for every child who deserves the opportunity to excel," he said. "You go on and do what's necessary to move on and contribute to society…and pass laws and bills and legislation that can be transformative."

He says every child deserves the chance to live up to their highest human potential. "Just give them hope. Just give them the chance," he said. "Whenever someone has given me a chance, I've always exceeded expectations. But if you never get the chance…sometimes you have to fight just to get the damn chance. That's the challenge in life."

"Soul City was meant to be part of that—to give people a decent life, with decent jobs and the opportunity to excel. Did we get there? No. Did we make progress? Yes. Does it give you hope? Absolutely. Does it mean something at the proper time under proper circumstances, something like Soul City could succeed?" he asked.

"Yes," he answered.

The original dream of Soul City may not have come true, but despite all of the challenges he's faced, McKissick believes the story of Soul City still makes a difference.

With the economic struggles in 2025, and with so much development driving up cost of living in the nearby Triangle area, he also believes Soul City could spark a new dream. The infrastructure from the 1970s is all still out there, just waiting to grow into an affordable bedroom community within commuting distance from the Triangle.

"I'm optimistic. I think we will see growth and development in Soul City. It's just a matter of somebody seeing that vision," he said. "Time will tell."

Chapter 4

UMSTEAD PARK

Ruins of a Rural Community Hidden Off Hiking Trails

Imagine strolling down the hiking trails of your city's most popular state park on a bright, sunny afternoon. You're chatting animatedly with your friend about the latest season of your favorite television show, waving at all the other hikers and taking in the beautiful fall scenery.

"Look at this little overgrown offshoot trail," I said to my friend. "I wonder where it goes? Maybe an older part of the park? Let's check it out!"

That's how we stumbled unexpectedly on an overgrown 1800s graveyard—tilted headstones with carvings so faded we couldn't read the names; sunken graves where the caskets beneath had begun deteriorating.

Our pulses quickened. Why was a graveyard in the middle of this beautiful, modern state park?

At the time, I hadn't yet learned that graveyards and cemeteries are hidden all over the place in North Carolina. They're tucked away in neighborhoods and hidden beneath mall parking lots, and many of our largest state parks have not only graves but also remains from homesites, gristmills, schools, churches, and even ghost gardens from long ago.

From that afternoon on, I was fascinated with the mystery of what happened to the lost community that once lived in the woods of modern-day William B. Umstead State Park.

Following: Page Mill, one of several mills along the former Crabtree Creek community, was already in decline in 1938. *Courtesy of Library of Congress, photographer Frances Johnston.*

Secret Ruins and Graves Hidden Deep in the Woods

Reggie King, descendant of one of the main families that once made up this small farming community, once told me, "Anywhere you see tulips or a large oak tree, that's where someone's front yard used to be."

When the first farmers arrived on the land around Crabtree Creek, which flows through the park even today, they settled into a hard way of life. Much of the gravelly land was inhospitable to crops, and the waters would rage during heavy rain, eventually washing away the beloved Company Mill. Oral history tells tales of both adults and children working hard on the farm, with some teens missing school for a year at a time. Eventually, after sustaining a community for generations, the rocky soil had given up all the nourishment it could, and the farmers eventually left the land after the Great Depression.

In its heyday, however, there were also many wonderful memories of a simpler time and a community-oriented way of life. Children recall making up their own woodland games and taking long walks in the forest with family. A kind shopkeeper sold candy for a penny or a nickel, and teachers worked closely with students in the community's school. The Company Mill became a social gathering place for gossip, and church brought everyone together on Sunday.

Left: The Carpenter family cemetery is just one graveyard hidden in the woods around modern-day William B. Umstead State Park. *Author's personal collection.*

Opposite: Remains of a stone chimney and foundation deep in the woods at Umstead Park. *Author's personal collection.*

Hidden Homesteads: Chimneys, Staircases, and Foundations Mark the Spot

When you look at the nearly 5,600 acres of heavily wooded land, camps, and hiking trails at Umstead Park today, it's hard to believe you're standing in the middle of a once bustling community. The ruins dotting the landscape today aren't obvious—until you know where to look. Passionate historians and even park rangers have spent countless hours searching for old homesites, creating maps, and clearing out trails to make them easier to reach.

Today, the Graylin Trail marks one "neighborhood road" that winds through multiple homesites and family cemeteries, many of which are not visible from the trail but can be found in the woods nearby. Today, most homesites are marked by piles of flat stones where foundations once held up grand farmhouses from the 1800s. Hikers can stand inside the "four walls" marked by foundation stones. From "inside" the home, take a look at the woods around you; it's like a glimpse back in time to what the families in this community saw every day.

Even in places where the foundation stones are scattered, the chimneys often survived. Sit beside the old stone fireplaces and imagine sleeping in

your cozy farmhouse on a cold winter night, listening to the sounds of the forest around you.

For hikers unaware of the land's history, it must be strange to unexpectedly spy a lone fireplace and chimney sitting in the woods or a toppled stone staircase coming out of the ground. True to Reggie's word, if you stand inside the old stone foundations and look around, you will often spy the two markers he described: an antique oak, trunk three times as thick as a person, standing guard over the family homestead, loyal through the generations; and a small patch of tulips, blooming as part of a ghost garden where the home's front porch once stood.

One particularly well-kept homesite, belonging to the Brown family, is hidden deep off trail in the woods. There, you'll find a tall stone wall in good condition—probably the chimney and fireplace—standing alongside another stone wall that's been crushed beneath a large fallen oak. Perhaps it was the oak that once marked their front yard.

Intermingled with broken branches and overgrowth, you'll find a grassy field of rusty farm equipment, sheets of metal buried in debris, useless buckets without any bottoms, glass bottles full of dirt, and old fences standing so long that they've grown straight into tree trunks. We even found wrought handmade nails, possibly crafted in the early 1800s. Some of the artifacts were barely recognizable, distorted by time.

The King Homestead

For some people living today, these old chimneys and disheveled piles of stones are far more than just ruins—they're home.

The ruins of the old King homesite look very different today than they did in the 1800s. The house was two stories tall, quite grand for its time and much larger than many of the other wooden cabins around the Crabtree Creek community.

When Reggie King looks at the old black-and-white photo of the King homesite, he sees a reflection of himself. The home belonged to William Allison "Al" King, born in 1829.

"Al King is my great-great-great-grandfather," said Reggie, looking at a photo of his ancestor, tall and well-dressed, one of the most prominent and wealthy men in the area. The King resemblance is still strong generations later.

"He owned over four hundred acres of land along Crabtree Creek. Today, that would be more than half the park!"

A photo of the King family homestead in its heyday. Today, only a small foundation and pieces of the stone chimney remain. *Courtesy of the King family.*

The photo, which hangs on the wall of the Umstead Park Visitor's Center today, shows the King family reunion gathered outside the grand old house. Dozens of people were in attendance. Generations later, the King family was still gathering at the old homesite—standing around the stone ruins in the woods.

"He had thirteen children sired between two marriages," laughed Reggie. "No wonder there's so many of us today!"

Kevin Doggett, also a descendent of Al King, remembers the family reunions. "We had family reunions out there. Last one we had out there was probably 2001. It was right before my grandparents passed away," he said. "We did it every year. It was tradition."

Even as a child, when Doggett visited Umstead Park with Boy Scouts, he always wondered if he was walking the same trails as his ancestors.

"We camped out there all the time, and I knew my family had been all over that park," he recalled. "When I'd camp out there, I'd wonder if I was sitting where my own family had sat. I was probably right in their footsteps and didn't even know it."

As he got older, the family reunions came to mean more and more. With all the growth and development around here, Doggett realized most families aren't able to pinpoint and visit the actual homesite of their ancestors that far back. "I felt fortunate," he said. "Just the fact that we were still willing to get together in that same place. You don't have a whole

The King family cemetery is one of the more prominent burial grounds remaining within Umstead Park. *Author's personal collection.*

lot of families who are able to do that. It's just awesome that we can still have those roots laid there."

During their last family reunion, Doggett stood inside the old stone foundation in front of the fireplace. He even found the daffodils that marked the front garden.

"Walking in there, just knowing that my family lived here," he said. "It means a lot."

Reggie says not many people can say they've stood inside the ruins of their great-great-great-grandfather's home.

"For me, it's kind of a spiritual thing to be honest with you. You feel like you've got a connection with the people who were there before you. It's emotional sometimes," he said. "You wish you could have known these people. You wish you could talk to these people."

The Company Mill: Largest Ruin in the Park Was Central to Community

It was around 1810 when Anderson Page built a grain grinding mill on Crabtree Creek that would eventually become known as the Company Mill. The Page name is well known even today in Wake County, as Anderson's son Frank Page would eventually become the founder of the town of Cary in 1871.

While several other mills were eventually built along the creeks running across Umstead Park, the Company Mill was the largest, and for generations it stood as the center of community and commerce, economy and gossip. Towering at an impressive three stories high, the grand old mill had plenty of space for events. In its heyday, around forty families used the mill for grinding wheat and corn.

"Two roads led to the Company Mill, one from the north and one from the south. Commercially, mule-drawn wagons brought sacks of corn and wheat to the mill to be ground. By the 1920s, some folks were even driving

The Company Mill in its heyday, dominating the skyline of the Crabtree Creek community. *Courtesy of the State Archives of North Carolina.*

their trucks to the mill to have grain ground," wrote the Friends of Page-Walker, a historic preservation group based in Cary.

When the business day was done, local farmers enjoyed gathering for parties, music, and dancing in the main room of the mill. They'd sit along the shore in the mill's shade and enjoy picnics.

In those days, the high water of Crabtree Creek pushed against the fifteen-foot-tall mill wall, creating a pond that acted as a local swimming hole. It's fitting, then, that today the Company Mill's sturdy stone wall remains as the largest ruin in the park. Even today, the Company Mill's remains are a cornerstone of community, where crowds gather on sunny spring days to play in the waterfall-like rapids, tiptoe through the swirling eddies, and sit on sun-warmed stones along the far side of the mill wall. How incredible that generations after the mill washed away, families are still gathering to swim and have picnics by the old mill wall—perhaps not even realizing the history hidden right under their noses.

The remaining wall stretches across the creek along the popular Company Mill Trail. Hikers can walk across the wall like a bridge or shamble down a hillside to get a closer look from the ground up. If you cross the creek and continue walking along the trail, you'll eventually find the Company Mill's millstone resting along the trail, honored by a historic marker.

The Company Mill was the beating heart of the surrounding farming community—a gathering place for social events and shopping. Today, only the stone wall remains. *Courtesy of the State Archives of North Carolina.*

The Night Company Mill Fell

So what happened to this grand old mill? Sadly, but not surprisingly, the Company Mill shared the common fate of many mills. Most mills are lost to one of two elements: fire or water.

If you notice, most of North Carolina's historic mills are no longer standing. Made of wood and lit with candles, many mills went up in flame as families looked on helplessly. Sitting on the shores of major waterways, most other mills washed away in floods.

Joe Grissom remembers the night the Company Mill fell. He shared the story in an oral history recorded at Umstead Park.

"It had been raining for a couple of days," recalled Grissom. "And back then, with a couple of days of moderate rain—or even heavy rain for just a short time—Crabtree Creek would 'get up,' as we said."

The Grissom home sat on top of a hill overlooking the mill down below. Grissom's father grew concerned after all the rain and decided to walk down and check on the dam site and see how the mill looked.

"I remember him coming back home, and he was all wet. He was standing on the rocks above the mill and one of the rocks gave way. He fell and was injured on the rocks below," said Grissom.

His father said, "If it keeps up like this, the mill won't be there in the morning."

The next morning, he and his father walked down the hill to the mill site. The Company Mill was gone.

"I saw nothing," said Grissom. "The mill crashed and washed away."

Seeing photos of the Company Mill, it's hard to believe a building so grand could simply vanish—not only from the skyline but from our memories. Today, the old stone wall and millstone are all that remain. Even the Grissom home is gone now, leaving barely a foundation in its place.

Life Along Crabtree Creek

Long before the first European settlers arrived in Wake County, modern-day state parks like Umstead, the Eno River, and the Dismal Swamp—each of which we will explore in this book—were home to Indigenous tribes. It wasn't until the 1700s that the first European settlers finally began farming in Wake County.

A small child stands among the fields of the former Crabtree Creek community. *Courtesy of the Library of Congress.*

Some of the earliest European families to begin farming on Umstead Park's land were the Warren, Page, Dillard, and Blake families. Shortly after, the King family settled the area, becoming one of the wealthiest families in the area. The earliest European farmers subsisted in a somewhat harsh landscape, living off the bounty of the forest, likely hunting deer, turkey, rabbits, and squirrels.

Eventually, the first farmers would attempt to tame a wilderness that was not ideal for farming. Buck Haley, who worked the land himself, said the land was rocky and hard. "This was rough farming country," he said. "It'd work you to death."

Even today, the sloped landscape and craggy soil provide an obvious clue to the struggles farmers would have faced. Regardless, in the 1800s and early 1900s, those woods were full of cozy wooden farmhouses with stone chimneys, complete with little gardens and fields of corn, wheat, and cotton.

In an oral history collected at Umstead Park, Agatha King Johnson recalled her time growing up along Crabtree Creek. She said it meant working hard—but also having fun adventures in the woods with the other kids. "We never got a day off work," she said. "Papa found something every day of his life for us to do."

Even on rainy days, Johnson said they had work. "You got in that corncrib and changed the corn from one side to the other," she recalled. "And you killed mice and rats. We had corn shuckings, and of course we had a corn sheller in there."

Her family raised cotton, corn, and hay. Other kids' chores on nearby farms could include milking cows or feeding the hogs. "We didn't get no rest. We'd like to have had a day off," she said.

Despite all the hard work, Johnson did admit to having a little fun now and again. "Gully Bug," she said. "You ever heard talk of Gully Bug? We had a place over in the woods, a deep, deep ravine, you know, we called the Gully. One would get in the bottom of that Gully, and he was the troll. You had to cross the Gully and not let this thing get you."

Johnson said the Gully's banks were "just as slick as they could be," worn away from the pitter-patter of happy children running up and down.

They also played children's classics like hopscotch and ball. But most of all, she said she loved taking walks in the woods. "Sometimes Momma would take us all and walk in the woods. Just walk in the woods," she remembered fondly. "Now we loved that."

One woman recalled the quiet, simple times from childhood at her grandmother's farmhouse in the fall. "Grandma Savannah and a couple more ladies, they'd come and stay a couple of hours and quilt," said Joyce Poole. "The quilt frame was hung down from the ceiling, and I could actually crawl under it. Sit under it and watch the needle come down through the material, and the four ladies would reach under and push it back down from the top. I'd sit an hour and done that. Just crawled around on the floor in different spots and just sit and look up at the needles. Mostly they was quiet, and sometimes they'd talk about somebody in the neighborhood who was sick."

Brothers Bill and Wiley Haley remember loading their little wagon with milk as kids and pulling it up Sycamore Creek to sell it at Dickinson's store for a nickel or a dime. Then they'd turn around and use that money to stuff their pockets with three big chocolate bars.

"If we had a nickel or a dime, we could go knock on Mrs. Dickinson's door, and she would go open the store and never complain about it," said Wiley.

"She'd walk across the road, open up that store. I've been over there for a penny, even. A penny piece of candy," added Bill.

Truma Warren Edgerton said even back then, you had to watch out for practical jokes from the other kids. "My sister used to love to milk the cow," she smiled. "And we'd be running around messing, and the worst thing—she would squirt out a milk stream and hit you in the face with it when she got a chance."

Historians have worked to preserve the memories and stories from the lost farming community at Umstead Park. With almost nothing left of the community itself, those memories are all that keep it alive.

"It's a good life," smiled Edgerton. "If I had my time to go over, I'd love to be on that farm and be outdoors with nature and all that again."

The End of the Crabtree Creek Farming Community

By the 1930s, the already challenging soil along Crabtree Creek had become drained of nutrients. It was eventually dubbed sub-marginal and no longer suitable for farming.

Around the same time, the mills along the creek also began closing, unable to compete with modern equipment.

By June 1935, offers to sell averaged out to around $11.30 per acre. At the time, the national average was around $10.00 per acre, so this was considered very fair by Land Program officials.

Ruins of homesteads can be found all around the woods at Umstead Park. The Brown Homestead, deeper in the woods, has rusting farm equipment left behind. *Author's personal collection.*

In the 1930s and early '40s, most families were moving out of the area. The Works Progress Administration (WPA) and Civilian Conservation Corps (CCC) began tearing down the farms and homesites, rendering the former Crabtree Creek farming community completely unrecognizable.

This would have been considered a win-win situation at the time. Farmers were able to sell their land, which was no longer workable, and move elsewhere. Meanwhile, the WPA and CCC were able to provide much-needed jobs during the Great Depression. Some farmers stayed in the area to work at the camps, and the area became known as the Crabtree Creek Recreation Demonstration Area.

In the wake of World War II, the federal programs were halted altogether. Some remnants of the CCC site stonework and bridges are still visible in the park today, becoming another layer of hidden history at Umstead Park.

In 1943, the federal government sold the land to the State of North Carolina for one dollar. By the 1950s, the park had been segregated. The state renamed the southern portion Reedy Creek State Park, with the northern portion renamed for Governor William Umstead. Eventually, in the 1960s, the park was re-combined into William B. Umstead State Park. Even today, the park has two entrances, serving as a modern-day reminder of its former segregation.

Voices from the Past

Descendants of the original Crabtree Creek families work to keep their memories alive today. Over the decades, historians have conducted oral histories with people who grew up on that land. Even the employees and rangers who oversee the park today get excited when asked about the old ruins hidden out in those woods. If you ask nicely, they may even give you a map to help you explore for yourself.

Because of the work being done to save those stories, people like Reggie King and Kevin Doggett can hear the voice of their great-grandmother—a woman they've never met.

"Rebecca King Jones, buried right there in Ebenezer Church cemetery by the park. There are recordings of her singing in the Smithsonian," explained Reggie. Her folk music song "Barbara Allen" is in the movie *Deliverance*.

"Who would have thought? You've been dead over one hundred years and your song is plastered all over the Internet? My great-grandmother is singing to people she's never met before, generations later. And even her descendants can still hear her voice."

Despite the work being done to keep the history of the little farming community alive, there are still thousands of people who hike through the woods each year, never even realizing the stories they're tromping over.

"I wish I could talk to Al King and my ancestors," said Reggie. "Stories and memories get watered down as time passes."

But overall, he thinks his family would be pleased—and perhaps a bit surprised—to see their little farming community has been remembered all these years later.

"I think they'd be happy that so many people are enjoying the land," he said. "I don't think they ever would have imagined it'd be what it is now. But their cemeteries are still cared for. They're still being talked about."

Most of all, they haven't been forgotten.

Chapter 5

SNOW CAMP

Crumbling Colonial Settlement Was a Stop on the Underground Railroad

The winding roads of rural North Carolina can take you to some unexpected places. Tucked away among those quiet curves and cotton fields are the humble remains of a Quaker settlement dating back over 250 years—and a hidden stop on the Underground Railroad.

The ramshackle wooden buildings, some tilting sideways under the weight of their own age and decay, are full of stories older than the United States itself. Here in the unincorporated community of Snow Camp, modern-day North Carolina vanishes in your rear view mirror as you step into the old South—a place where small farmers and Quakers first battled for freedom from Britain and later pushed to see enslaved people gain freedom, too.

A gathering of single-room log cabins—many with dilapidated doorways falling off their hinges—circles a central water tower. An antique post office sits frozen in time, full of old sorting tables and trays. Next door, a one-room schoolhouse—complete with antique desks, a chalkboard, a threadbare map, and even a central wood stove—provides a glimpse into how children learned in centuries past. A sign by the door reads "Colored School House."

One squat wooden structure, perhaps the oldest in the area, is marked as the original 1751 Cane Creek Meeting House, home of the first Quaker congregation in Snow Camp.

This collection of empty, dilapidated buildings may look like a ghost town at first glance, but this vacant community is not the result of lost history but of saved history.

Ruins of a Quaker settlement dating back to the 1700s can be found in Snow Camp. *Author's personal collection.*

Whereas many rural communities explored in this book watched their history vanish piece by piece—or perhaps wash away all at once—Snow Camp is a different story. Two men by the names of James and Robert Wilson purchased this piece of land where they could protect and preserve historic buildings from the surrounding area. In saving history, they essentially created a "ghost town" museum. The historic buildings, many that were slated to be torn down, were rescued and moved to a slice of land where they could be protected and even explored by visitors. Locals describe the brothers as "hoarders of history," saying there was never an old building they didn't want.

Because of their work, Snow Camp is one of the few places in North Carolina where you can find tangible remnants of the Underground Railroad.

Bloody Revolutionary Battles in the Quaker Belt

Although Snow Camp looks peaceful today, there was a time when war and death ravaged this idyllic landscape.

In the 1740s, the first European settlers began wandering into the wooded area now known as Snow Camp. According to legend, it was wintertime when hunters and trappers arrived, setting up camp in the deep snow. From then on, the area was referred to as the "Snow Camp."

Local tradition says this "Snow Camp" was around a fourth of a mile from where the Cane Creek Meeting House would eventually be built in 1751.

Top: This small cabin has a sign reading "Cane Creek Meeting House." The original Cane Creek Meeting House was built in 1751. *Author's personal collection.*

Bottom: The small Quaker community of Snow Camp played a major role in the Revolutionary War and, later, the Underground Railroad. *Author's personal collection.*

Small Farmers Begin Rumblings of Rebellion

Small, single-room log cabins began popping up along Cane Creek, along with the meeting house and Dixon's Mill. The whole region would eventually become known as the Quaker's Belt, with other communities like New Garden, Deep River, and Centre being established nearby.

"For many years life among the Quakers who had settled along Cane Creek was peaceful. Farmers tilled their fields; the blacksmith hammered at his forge; Simon Dixon kept his mill wheel turning; bonneted women and black-hatted men went to meeting on First Day," described Bobbie T. Teague in the book *Cane Creek: Mother of Meetings*.

These early communities were mostly small homesteads getting by with subsistence farming. Cane Creek couldn't support industrial-sized farms or mills. The yeoman farmers grew corn, oats, and wheat.

Despite being a peaceful Quaker community, some early seeds of revolution were planted along Cane Creek.

An artistic depiction of the first Cane Creek Meeting House. It was extremely small compared to most modern-day meetinghouses—and even the newer ones are still relatively humble. *Courtesy of the Cane Creek Meeting.*

Royal Governor William Tryon dreamed of building himself a wildly expensive palace—and began reaching into the pockets of backcountry farmers to help afford it. Corruption and greed seeped into land transactions, as Tryon even went so far as to trick farmers into believing their property deeds were invalid. Farmers who couldn't pay the skyrocketing taxes could find their crops or livestock confiscated.

"Homes were invaded and any silverware, fine china, or precious hand-woven linen and woolen goods brought from the old country were taken despite the desperate and tearful protests of grief-stricken housewives," wrote Teague.

The farmers' desperation gave rise to the Regulator Movement, an early rebellion that helped spark the later Revolutionary War. While multiple farmers in Snow Camp would have supported the movement, there were three names that stood out as instigators in Cane Creek: Herman Husband, William Cox, and Simon Dixon.

Husband, one of the principal spokespeople for the movement, wrote rebellious tracts to help fire up the population. In 1768, only a few years before the Revolutionary War began, Governor Tryon received a report that hundreds of men had gathered at Simon Dixon's Mill with a plan to march into Hillsborough and burn it down.

While this plan was averted, tensions continued rising, finally culminating in the Battle of Alamance in 1771—a deadly fight between two thousand Regulators and Tryon's militia—which some historians have argued was the "first battle of the Revolutionary War."

Revolution: War and Death Arrive in a Peaceful Community

Even deep down the backroads of rural North Carolina, the rumbles of war would be felt. However, Quakers tried to continue their peaceful, quiet, and spiritual way of life.

General Charles Cornwallis was marching his troops across the state, camping at mills along the way.

Dixon's Mill had been punished after the Battle of Alamance, with Tryon taking additional supplies after winning the fight. Dixon was nervous his mill would be targeted by British troops during their march to Wilmington—and sure enough, Cornwallis took a less-direct route and went out of his way to camp at Dixon's.

Sadly, although Dixon escaped to Moncure ahead of a warning that the British were coming, he returned home too soon and was taken captive. He died shortly after; many believe he was tortured.

STANDING INSIDE DIXON'S MILL TODAY

Today, the remains of Dixon's Mill are a crumbling stone wall stretching along the roadside. Once a grand sight on the horizon, towering multiple stories over the grassy hillside, this wall would have been surrounded by small Quaker homes and farms.

Stand beside the wall and take a look around. You can envision Cornwallis's two thousand troops camping in the grassy field, lighting hundreds of campfires against the cold. You can imagine the hopelessness the Quakers must have felt.

The soldiers drained the residents of resources, slaughtering hundreds of sheep, cows, and other livestock for their dinner. Sick and injured soldiers took over the Cane Creek Meeting House, which sat on property donated by Dixon himself.

Similar to the story of Brunswick Town, described earlier in this book, the little Quaker community of Snow Camp was another spark on the powder keg of the American Revolution. Like in Brunswick Town, the residents paid the price—but this would not be the last time the peaceful community stood up in the face of danger and war.

UNDERGROUND RAILROAD

After standing up against tyranny ahead of the Revolutionary War, the Quaker community stood up once again before the Civil War.

Ron Osborne, a historian and storyteller whose family roots go back ten generations in Quaker Belt soil, says the Quaker community has historically been active in matters of justice and human rights, starting hundreds of years ago and stretching all the way into modern times. Even today, the Spring Friends Meeting, where he attends, is involved in trying to improve society.

"For centuries, a swath of land in these rural areas of Alamance, Guilford, Forsyth, Randolph, and part of Orange County were a bastion of liberal and progressive social movements like the Underground Railroad and antiwar movement," he said. "The Quaker Belt."

Quaker communities and meeting houses in the area included New Garden, Cane Creek, Spring Friends, Deep River, and Centre.

"Word would get out to freedom seekers that if they could make it to the Quaker Belt, they could find help," explained Osborne. "If they could find an area populated by Quakers, they could find a friendly population."

Alongside the Quaker community, the region had a population of free Black families that also helped freedom seekers in their journey north.

Tangible Remnants of the Underground Railroad Still Standing in the Quaker Belt

The road to freedom was extremely dangerous—and it looked different depending on which direction a freedom seeker headed. Some freedom seekers followed rivers, known as freedom roads, toward the coast, hoping to catch a boat north or vanish into the Great Dismal Swamp, where Maroon colonies had been established by free Black communities. Other freedom seekers headed toward the Quaker Belt, hoping to find a conductor on the

The Quaker Belt of North Carolina was full of meeting houses. This one dates back to the 1800s. *Author's personal collection.*

Underground Railroad to provide them with supplies, a helping hand, and a safe hiding place.

"Snow Camp would have had a station, and the next station could be up in Centre, and then they'd travel to New Garden or Mendenhall Plantation," said Osborne.

Freedom seekers would often travel in cover of darkness. During the day, they'd hide in someone's home, often in a crawlspace or secret area. Richard Mendenhall, a Quaker who owned a plantation, was actively involved in the Underground Railroad. Today, visitors can explore the historic site, which still has an original false-bottom wagon used to smuggle freedom seekers to safety.

The false-bottom wagon was driven by Quaker teenagers as young as thirteen carrying loads of fine Carolina pottery covered with hay. Andrew Murrow and Isaac Stanley, two of the primary drivers, would often travel back and forth from North Carolina to Ohio or Indiana. Curled up quietly in a hidden compartment, barely daring to breathe, freedom seekers would pray to make it safely up north without getting caught. For the abolitionist Quakers, getting caught could mean losing their farm, going to jail, or facing physical harm. For the freedom seekers, getting caught could mean returning to slavery, going to jail, physical torture, or even death.

Another remnant of the Underground Railroad is in the former community of New Garden, today known as Guilford College. Down a series of hiking trails and deep into the woods, visitors can find a section of old-growth forest not yet destroyed by development. Historic documents indicate one specific tree—standing far taller and broader than the rest—was a resting place for freedom seekers traveling through the Quaker Belt. Known today as the Underground Railroad Tree, its shelter offered protection, far enough from prying eyes but close enough to the Quaker school to receive supplies and food from the students.

One station on the Underground Railroad was only about one and a half miles away from the Cane Creek meeting house in the home of William Kirkman. "He had a two-story log house, the upstairs of which was large enough to use as a dining room and also a sleeping room when there was no immediate threat from their pursuers," wrote Teague in *Cane Creek: Mother of Meetings*. "During the day, they hid in a large hollow log some distance from the house. Only when it was dark and deemed to be safe would they venture into the house to eat and rest."

There was no map to the Underground Railroad. The network of stations was very loosely connected. One conductor might only know where the next station was, and nothing beyond that, so if anyone got caught, everyone else down the tracks would still be safe. Secret codes and songs were used to help guide freedom seekers along their path. For example, carefully hidden nails would be driven into trees in a specific pattern to help point the way.

Songs like "Follow the Drinkin' Gourd," "Go Down, Moses," and "Swing Low, Sweet Chariot" are connected with the Underground Railroad. A freedom seeker hiding in the brush would listen carefully, as an abolitionist singing an innocent song as they walk past may be secretly offering "instructions" on which way to go next.

Teacher at New Garden Boarding School Nearly Killed for Work on Underground Railroad

A number of students, teachers, and faculty at New Garden Boarding School played a role in the Underground Railroad and abolitionist movement.

Osborne's direct ancestor was one of those teachers. "He was a conductor on the Underground Railroad," said Osborne. "His name was Needham Perkins."

In the 1840s, more than twenty years before the Civil War, Perkins opened his home to freedom seekers. "He would build a big roaring fire some nights and open the door and usher in freedom seekers to dry out their clothes and get warm," said Osborne. "The next morning, they were all hidden, and the next night he'd get them all to the next station."

After the Civil War, he became an officer in the Federal Freedmen's Bureau, an agency charged with helping support the Black community as they assimilated into society.

But not everyone agreed with Perkins's work. "Reconstruction was a very ugly time," said Osborne. "One night, he got off the train and was walking home, and he was approached in the dark by two men. One man called out his name and pistol whipped him in the head. As he fell to the ground, they took out a knife, slit his throat, and left him to die."

Perkins somehow survived, regaining consciousness and staggering home. He died a few years later.

"He never did say who his assailants were," said Osborne. "He never named them."

Not All Quakers Supported the Underground Railroad

"Not all Quakers were abolitionists, and not all helped with the Underground Railroad," explained Osborne. "It was a big debate among our community."

Some Quakers felt they needed to follow the law—and helping freedom seekers escape was breaking a legal order. Others said it was acceptable to disobey laws in order to do what was morally right. Some remained neutral, not taking a side.

Some Quakers even held enslaved people. Richard Mendenhall, whose plantation holds the false-bottom wagon used to help freedom seekers escape, had a younger brother who had one of the largest slave holdings in Guilford County. Like some other Quakers, he inherited them, and although he supported the abolitionist movement and Underground Railroad, he kept ownership papers for some time.

Freeing an enslaved person could be dangerous in the South. Even if they were free, they could be picked up and enslaved again. Some records show enslaved men actually asking Mendenhall to purchase them, as they knew

Historic buildings from around the Quaker Belt were brought to the Snow Camp Outdoor Theater, where they have been preserved. *Author's personal collection.*

he'd be kind and wouldn't send them farther south away from their families. Some abolitionist Quakers kept enslaved people in order to legally protect them until they could be safely freed in the North.

John Newlin, a member of the Spring Friends Meeting who built the original mill at Saxapahaw on the Haw River, held forty-two people in slavery after inheriting them from his neighbor under the condition that they would be carried to freedom over the Ohio River. "But her relatives contested it, and for ten years, there was an injunction where he could not take his charges to freedom," said Osborne. "He had to keep them in the county while it went through the court system. Finally, after ten years, he won the case and was able to finally lead them all up into Indiana and had them set free."

Even the Quakers' North Carolina Yearly Meeting accepted "ownership" of several enslaved people in order to protect them. They paid them wages for their labor and ensured they would not be separated from their families. These people were known as the "Quaker Free Negroes," according to Teague.

As a whole, the Quaker community expressed "grave concern" over the practice of slavery. Members who attempted to enslave a person could be disowned, and a good number of members involved themselves in helping freedom seekers.

Pre-Revolutionary and Antebellum Ruins in Snow Camp

Unlike many communities, Snow Camp has managed to stay connected to its history and roots.

Some of that history has been reduced to ruins, but thanks to the Quaker meeting houses and a pair of brothers with a love of preservation, Snow Camp is home to a large collection of historic structures dating all the way back to the 1700s.

Simon Dixon's Mill and Simon Dixon's Wall

Dating back to the 1750s, the ruins of Simon Dixon's mill can still be seen along the roadside in Snow Camp. Owned by a leader of the Regulators—an early movement sparking the Revolutionary War—it became the site where Cornwallis's troops camped while marching through Alamance County.

A local legend contends that buried treasure could still be somewhere around the old mill. When warned the British were approaching his mill, Dixon reportedly stuffed his stockings full of gold and valuables and made his escape. According to a February 14, 1937 article in the *Winston-Salem Journal*, he then buried his treasure near a "rocky branch running towards the rising sun."

During the publication of that article, written nearly a century ago, Dixon's Mill was still operational. Today, however, the stones that made up the foundation are all that remain. You can see the outline of the mill down in the creek as you cross the bridge on Sylvan School Road.

Not far away is a long, rocky wall marked with a sign reading "Simon Dixon's wall." The sign dates the wall back to 1749, the year Simon Dixon arrived in Snow Camp.

Today, Simon and his wife, Elizabeth, are buried beneath a millstone in the Cane Creek Meeting Cemetery.

Cane Creek Friends and Spring Friends Meeting Houses

The Cane Creek Meeting House, first built in 1751, has seen multiple changes across the decades. The original meeting house looks like a tiny log cabin. Sketches from the 1800s show a more modern meeting house, with white panels and two entryways. Today, it stands as a simple but elegant brick building with a steeple and white pillars.

Down the road a bit, the Spring Friends Meeting House looks like a watercolor landscape painting—a simple country sanctuary sitting in a peaceful field, cut by a meandering stream and an idyllic little bridge. It's hard to believe that not far from here, over 250 soldiers lay bleeding and dying after the brutal Battle of Lindley's Mill in the Revolutionary War. Perhaps this landscape was the last sight they saw with their living eyes. The community's Quakers nursed the wounded from both sides of the battle and helped bury the dead in a mass grave.

The cemeteries for each of these meeting houses hold much of Snow Camp's history—generations of people who helped spark the Revolution and worked quietly in the Underground Railroad.

A modern-day look at the Cane Creek Meeting House. Compare it with the original wooden cabin built in 1751. *Author's personal collection.*

The Spring Friends Meeting House looks like a watercolor painting. They began meeting in 1761. *Author's personal collection.*

Snow Camp Outdoor Theater

Like any unincorporated rural community, Snow Camp has lost its share of historic buildings. However, thanks to the work of two brothers, a large portion of history from across the Quaker Belt has been saved all in one place.

"Snow Camp Outdoor Theater was the brainchild of James and Robert Wilson," recalled Osborne.

The theater was originally built to tell the story of the early lives of the Quakers in Snow Camp. "The drama *Sword of Peace* tells the story of Simon Dixon, the miller, and his wife Elizabeth. Their quiet Quaker lives are disrupted by events leading up to the Battle of Alamance....The drama culminates with Lord Cornwallis bringing his troops to Snow Camp," described Teague in *Cane Creek: The Mother of Meetings*.

Less than half a mile down the road, the ruins of Dixon's Mill quietly watch their story live on centuries later.

Snow Camp Outdoor Theater almost looks like a ghost town, holding remnants of the post office, an 1800s Friends meetinghouse, a water tower, a covered bridge, a one-room schoolhouse, and many other structures from the Quaker Belt. *Author's personal collection.*

Starting in 1994, another drama was added to the theater: *Pathway to Freedom*. This production tells the story of the Underground Railroad in Snow Camp.

"The community kind of coalesced around the theater," said Osborne. "It became a point of pride and community service and volunteerism. I was in the cast for four years, playing Levi Coffin, who is actually one of my ancestors in the Quaker Belt. All three of our kids were in the plays, too."

People began donating historic artifacts. "They donated knitting machines. Looms. Muskets. Gristmill machines," said Osborne. "And buildings. Some buildings came from as far away as Centre."

Today, the old buildings circle the parking lot, allowing visitors a chance to step back in time. James Wilson collected the New Hope Meeting House and the Chatham Meeting House, a post office, and an old one-room schoolhouse. "Probably around a third to half of the buildings were from Snow Camp itself," said Osborne.

Just down Drama Road, the burned remains of Ye Old Country Kitchen stand as a sad reminder to a piece of community history that could not be saved. "Oh, it was a community staple!" recalled Osborne. "We'd go down there once a week. Everyone would be there, especially in summertime."

In its heyday, Snow Camp Outdoor Theater was hosting full-scale productions four nights a week over the summertime. Sadly, some time after James Wilson's death, the theater began struggling. In 2020, the site had been closed for about a year—and it showed. The theater was overgrown, with plants growing up between the plastic seats, fallen leaves carpeting the stage, and broken wood scattered about. The owner explained the cost and work of maintaining the historic buildings was becoming too much, and some locals began to fear the theater would never recover.

As of 2025, a new studio has taken over, and Snow Camp Outdoor Theater has come to life once again. Crews have been fixing up buildings, cleaning the site, and decorating for the holidays. STUDIO 1, which has taken over productions, has been working hard to repair and rejuvenate the site. Osborne says the scale isn't quite as large as during the theater's prime due to budget issues. In order to preserve the rich history of Snow Camp, it seems vital that more people visit the theater and explore the old ghost town of vacant historic buildings—or else the story of Snow Camp will be forgotten, and it truly will become lost history.

Chapter 6

FROM LOST COVE TO PORTSMOUTH ISLAND

Ghost Towns of the Mountains, Islands, and Forests

If you've made it this far in the book, you know ghost towns and lost communities are hidden all across the Old North State. They're on top of mountains, deep beneath lakes, off wooded hiking trails, and even on abandoned islands.

Any time you're near a river, a prominent body of water, or even a man-made lake, it's likely you're tromping through the ground-down remains of a place where human beings once thrived. Even city parks are often built on land that once served as plantations, farms, schools, orphanages, or poor communities lost to urban renewal.

Many of these communities are in varying stages of decay. Some have been completely taken by nature or destroyed by developers, while others have just a few stone reminders of what once stood there. When it comes to ghost towns, most people are hoping to see more than just a few stones or foundations. So if you're hoping to explore larger remnants, like full houses, mills, shops, and churches from the 1800s, here are some of the most visual ghost towns in the Old North State.

One is tucked away deep in Appalachia, accessible only after a long hike through the mountains. All the way across the state, another has been forgotten on an abandoned island. In the Piedmont, the Eno River is home to century-old wooden cabins that have been shielded from the elements for generations.

The best part—you can visit and tour all three of these ghost towns, and if you dare to sleep alongside the ghosts, you can even stay the night at some of them.

The Anthony Cole House looks straight out of a scene from *Little House on the Prairie*, surrounded by a grassy cove and yellow daffodils. *Author's personal collection.*

Lost Cove

One of the most legendary ghost towns in Appalachia, Lost Cove has been isolated from civilization ever since it was first built in the 1860s. There are no roads leading to the community, only hiking trails deep into the remote mountains and dense forest of Yancey County. Disconnected from the outside world, the settlement, which never had access to electricity, survived by being as rugged and determined as the rocky landscape that birthed it. In fact, that isolation was the point of Lost Cove from the very beginning.

Stephen "Morgan" Bailey, who served for the Union during the Civil War, took refuge in the thick, mountainous woods along the Nolichucky River Valley, building his humble cabin along the border of North Carolina and Tennessee.

"Possibly he was trying to escape the ravages of the Civil War, which brought chaos to the mountains of Western North Carolina. This area was a constant (if non-formal) battleground: brothers fighting brothers, fathers against sons, and neighbors against neighbors," wrote historian Christy Smith after interviewing and collecting oral histories from families connected with the ghost town.

It was somewhat common for men, seeking to avoid taking a side in the war, to hide in the secret spaces of Appalachia. Linville Caverns, the only cave in North Carolina that allows public tours, was a hiding spot for both Union and Confederate soldiers. They lived together in the limestone caverns—enemy soldiers sharing a home while the war raged outside.

In time, the hidden haven of Lost Cove began to attract other settlers to the fertile mountainside. Just like the homesteaders of today, the community attracted families who wanted to be self-sufficient away from the modern world. Settlers left behind the secular amenities of well-established towns, instead growing their own crops and animals on quiet homesteads. Small wooden cabins, old barns, corncribs, sawmills, and smokehouses began to dot the rolling, grassy mountainsides.

For decades, the Lost Cove community thrived, shaping its own destiny. But in the 1950s, the final residents would leave the town behind—frozen in time, with furniture still in the houses and pots and pans still on the stove, as if they believed they'd someday return home again.

Ghost Town Hidden Deep in the Mountains

Today, Lost Cove is almost like the lost city of Atlantis for explorers—so many people want to see the legendary ghost town hidden deep in the woods of Appalachia.

As the town has been abandoned for about sixty years, the forest has begun to take it over. Most of the wooden cabins, hand built by the original settlers, are gone, leaving only stone foundations or stairways as markers. The remaining cabins are like a scene from a movie: dilapidated wooden structures, standing like quiet sentinels in a grassy clearing. A cracked windowpane or door frame, bent beneath years of decay, peering from behind a thick curtain of ivy. A towering stone chimney hidden amid the trees.

One of the most iconic scenes from Lost Cove is the rusted skeleton of a vintage 1938 Chevy slumped against a tree trunk like an exhausted wild animal that took one final rest—and never woke up. It once belonged to a resident named Swin Miller, who used it to drive workers and timber to and from the railroad. Today, many hikers snap photos of the iconic truck, never even realizing its story or importance to Lost Cove.

Along the crest of a grassy knoll is the Lost Cove Cemetery, where around two dozen graves wait for visits from loved ones who likely cannot visit often. None of the headstones are ornate; many were lovingly hand-carved by locals John Miller and Velmer Bailey. Some headstones have been lost completely. According to Smith, every resident of Lost Cove has a loved one buried in the cemetery. Even children were buried here, having lost their young lives after a typhoid outbreak reached the remote community.

To visit Lost Cove today, you must hike in, just as the settlers did so many years ago. In those days, residents hiked into and out of the Cove to access goods and services from nearby communities. The path into the ghost town is like a trail back through time, taking you along the old railroad tracks and riverbank settlers would have used as landmarks decades ago.

Because the ghost town is so overgrown and seldom visited, visitors should watch out for wildlife that has made its home in Lost Cove in the years since humans left.

LIFE IN LOST COVE

At its peak, about two hundred people lived in Lost Cove, and more than a dozen homes were scattered across the mountain. The neighboring families worked together to create a self-sufficient community way down the backroads of Appalachia.

Many of the families owned farms or mills and lived in simple log cabins, sleeping in beds made of straw and feathers, decorated with handmade quilts. With no electricity, families kept warm using stoves and fireplaces. They raised chickens and crops, with apples being an important moneymaker, according to Smith. Moonshine was also a popular "crop" for families in Lost Cove.

Being isolated, they relied on traveling doctors to come into town for medical emergencies. In the early days, these traveling doctors served well enough; however, as medical care grew more advanced in the mid-1900s, access to healthcare became one of the reasons people began leaving Lost Cove. Locals had to hike to the closest town in order to get access to things like doctors, shops, groceries, or mail.

Like many mountain communities, Lost Cove's culture centered on church. The picturesque chapel sat on a knoll above the town, where "it was seen from every house in the settlement," writes Smith. The one-room church also served as the schoolhouse. One local described the church as having "desks on one side and pews on the other side."

A profoundly spiritual community, the residents gathered for worship, singing hymns that filled the cove and bounced across the valley. They enjoyed regular church gatherings and revivals.

Just as they relied on traveling doctors, they also relied on traveling teachers to bring education from the outside world to the youth of Lost Cove. Smith says the teachers often boarded with the Tiptons or the Millers after arriving in Lost Cove by train.

"Their teachings helped the students learn about the outside world, and, in return, the outside world came to this little mountain school," Smith wrote.

LEAVING LOST COVE BEHIND

Unlike many ghost towns explored in this book, Lost Cove was protected from things like developers, war, and even natural disasters. So what could have possibly infiltrated this hidden forest haven and destroyed it from within?

It was the loss of self-reliance. Over time, the outside world gained comforts and essentials like electricity, indoor plumbing, heating and air conditioning, automobiles, better education, and advanced medical care. Certainly, the access to the additional safety and protection of modern communities would have been attractive to some families.

However, it was the railroad that spelled the beginning of the end for Lost Cove, according to Smith. The railroad had initially brought additional jobs and money, allowing Lost Cove families to benefit from their supply of timber and lumber mills and then load up the train and sell their products. However, after many years of cutting down forests and selling timber to surrounding communities, they finally began to run out of trees. This meant a source of money that depended heavily on the outside world had suddenly dried up.

"Lost Cove's earlier self-reliance had given way to dependence, and people wanted a new life in neighboring towns, new jobs, and new schools," wrote Smith.

The younger generation began leaving their small mountain settlement for the promise of better careers or quality education, and the older generation perhaps began seeking a more comfortable life in nearby cities or towns.

As each family left, one by one, it became even harder to live in Lost Cove. It was becoming a ghost town. The remaining families literally took what they could carry and hiked out of their homes.

Many left their furniture behind, creating a ghost town that seems eerily like everyone just vanished in the middle of daily life. Perhaps, in a way, that's exactly what happened. Many families believed they would return again someday—that life would return to Lost Cove.

Portsmouth Island

Just as the abandoned Henry River Mill Village is hidden in the mountains, the ghost town of Portsmouth is hidden on its own island. People passing by the island by boat will see a hazy outline of the church steeple in the distance. For those who step on the island's shores, however, there's far more to explore.

It is owned today by the National Park Service, and many of the buildings have been restored. For years, however, some of the vacant buildings had begun decaying in the salty ocean air.

The little island community, built in the 1700s before the Revolutionary War, appears frozen in time. Today, the old church, schoolhouse, post office,

Top: Portsmouth Village is a ghost town on an abandoned island. *Courtesy of National Park Service.*

Bottom: Henry Pigott House was one of the last remaining residents of Portsmouth Village in the 1960s. His family is directly descended from enslaved people who worked on the island. *Courtesy of National Park Service.*

and Coast Guard station are still standing. Some of the village houses also remain—simple, short, yellow homes with white pillars and small yards surrounded by white picket fences. Some structures are more intact than others, as there's far more variety in the architecture of this colonial port town than in the identical copy-and-paste homes of a mill village.

Visitors must catch a ferry or boat to explore the historic ghost town, but it is open for guests.

The beautiful white church with a towering black steeple strikes a pose along the tidal marshes, partially hidden behind long wisps of grass billowing in the breeze. Some of the magnificent old beach houses bear scars from withstanding decades of hurricanes.

One can imagine living on this island paradise and bustling port town during its heyday would have felt serene and exciting all at the same time.

But it wasn't serene for everyone.

Life in Portsmouth Village: Slavery in a Bustling Seaport

Established in 1753, Portsmouth Village is about 150 years older than Henry River Mill Village—and daily life here was far different.

Over the next two decades, Portsmouth grew into a major port, becoming one of the largest settlements along the Outer Banks. Hundreds, if not thousands, of cargo ships made port at Portsmouth as they headed through the Ocracoke Inlet.

The Theodore and Anne Salter House currently serves as the visitor center. *Courtesy of National Park Service.*

Because of the immense amount of demanding manual work, enslaved men were often used to load and unload the constant stream of cargo ships. Worse, some of the "cargo" was, in fact, more enslaved people. According to the National Park Service, "By 1830, Portsmouth's population was about 393 people, including 120 enslaved people."

Many more structures were built on the island that are no longer standing today. There were windmills, hospitals, and churches. The population ballooned to

An old illustration of the bustling port life in Portsmouth Village. *Courtesy of National Park Service.*

six hundred residents and over one hundred homes on the small island. A one-room schoolhouse was built in the early 1900s, and schoolteacher Mary Sneed Dixon began educating multiple grades at the same time.

By the early 1900s, the booming port town was starting to slow down. Residents began moving off the island, leaving empty homes behind. Abandoned buildings began to decay in the harsh environment. The hospital burned down, and two churches were destroyed in a hurricane.

"The closing of Portsmouth School sounded its death knell as a growing community," writes Connie Mason in *Portsmouth Remembered*. "Young families could no longer educate their children, so they moved off the island. Portsmouth was left with a population of older residents."

Fewer than twenty residents still lived on the island in 1950. Job opportunities were virtually nonexistent, and supplies had to be purchased on the mainland or brought by boat.

Just across the Ocracoke Inlet, the island village of Ocracoke was still going strong, with increasing levels of tourism—a sad reflection on a future Portsmouth would never see.

By 1971, the final remaining residents had left Portsmouth fully abandoned, leaving behind a real-life island ghost town.

Eno River: Cabins, Graves, and a NASCAR Speedway Hidden in the Woods

Be careful when stepping into the deep woods and steep terrain along the Eno River's banks; if you aren't careful, you could stumble right back in time to the 1700s.

Some scenes look straight from *Little House on the Prairie*—a two-hundred-year-old cabin, shockingly well-preserved after centuries of neglect, sitting in a grassy clearing with flowers and trees sprouting all around. Then, down another trail, a stone spring house that almost looks like a home to a magical creature. Walk a little more, and you'll stumble into an 1800s cemetery with sunken graves—with more than one spooky legend attached.

The land along the Eno River is full of crumbling mill walls, old brick fireplaces, and dilapidated wooden cabins in various stages of decay. There's

Above: The Anthony Cole House is just one decaying 1800s cabin hidden in the woods around the Eno River. *Author's personal collection.*

Following: Sister's House has caved in over the centuries. This home was built for Cole's sister in the 1800s. *Courtesy of Kelly Gomez,* The Forgotten South.

even the remains of an entire racetrack, which originated as a wealthy industrialist's horse-racing track at the turn of the century but eventually became a major NASCAR track in the 1940s. Deep along another hiking trail, you'll find labyrinthian ruins of a water pump station's basement carved deep into the hillside.

In short, the trails of the Eno River can take you to relics from multiple time periods—from the early 1800s all the way to the 1950s. The life-sustaining source of water served Indigenous tribes, such as the Eno and the Occaneechi, for generations. The valuable resource attracted settlers who moved into the area and built livelihoods—farms, mills, schools, and even plantations—along its banks.

Similar to William B. Umstead Park, the remains of those lost communities have been left behind for people to explore today; however, the ruins along the Eno River seem to be in better condition than those at Umstead. This is probably because many of the homesteads at Umstead were torn down when the CCC began building its camps.

The Eno River Valley almost suffered a similar fate to the New Hope River Valley, which was flooded to create Jordan Lake. In the 1960s, there was discussion about flooding the land along the Eno River to create a reservoir for the city of Durham. Fortunately, a passionate group of people came together to protect the land and its history, leaving behind a treasure-trove of historic structures from across the centuries.

West Point: Life Along the Eno River

European farmers and millers began settling along the Eno River as early as the mid-1700s. At one point, more than thirty mills were active along the stretch of river near modern-day Durham; while most of them have long since been washed away by time, there are ruins throughout the woods. A large mill still dominates the skyline at West Point on the Eno, which served as the heart of the river valley's community in the 1800s. It's not the original mill, which collapsed from old age; however, the replica serves its purpose as a window to how the world may have looked back then.

According to the Eno River Association, which protects and preserves the land's history and natural resources, "The mill was the vital center for a thriving community of about 300 families."

This central area also had a general store, a blacksmith shop, a cotton gin, a sawmill, and a post office.

Historian Jean Anderson, who wrote a seminar on life in a mill community, reported that the West Point miller was paid only $150 in 1870, which was not considered a good wage. Prior to the Civil War, enslaved men were often used to run the mills. Wealthy local families like the Bennehan family, who owned Stagville Plantation, and the Cameron family, who owned a plantation in Raleigh, used unpaid enslaved labor for the mills they owned along the Eno. Stagville Plantation still stands today, not far from the Eno River.

Just like Company Mill in Umstead or Dixon's Mill in Snow Camp, the mill at West Point served as the social hub for the community of farming families that were scattered along the river's shores. Here at the mill, they could get new clothes, furniture, meat, whiskey, and playing cards, as well as groceries and medicine.

After Durham was founded in 1869, it began drawing from the Eno River Valley community for resources—including water. In 1887, the city had a water pump station constructed along the river. Today, the pump station ruins are among the most sizable remains for explorers to visit. As the city grew, many of the prominent men in the river community began shifting their wealth and political power to Durham. They ran for mayor and city council and brought their businesses closer to the city. Likewise, the economic power of mills began declining after the Industrial Revolution, pushing families to move to the burgeoning city that offered far more opportunities.

Anthony Cole House and Sister's House

Sitting in the middle of a grassy grove, surrounded by dancing yellow blooms of daffodils, is a two-hundred-year-old settler's cabin with wide open doors and caved-in wooden floors. The Anthony Cole House appears like a ghost in the woods, barely visible through the trees as you wander along the dusty trails.

There was a time when homes like this were a common sight in the Eno River Valley.

Overgrown with vines and tall grass, one side of the modest home sags beneath the weight of its age. A peek through the wilting door frame reveals a hollow room with solid logs stretched from one side to another and the rocky foundation visible underneath. The other side of the home is faring a bit better, with floorboards still covering the logs below.

A peek inside a two-hundred-year-old home belonging to the Cole family. *Author's personal collection.*

Sister's House was much smaller than Anthony Cole's. The Cole family had more than a dozen children, but "Sister" likely lived alone. *Courtesy of Kelly Gomez,* The Forgotten South.

A floating staircase leads to a second floor. The hovering steps clearly once attached in an L-shape to wooden bottom steps, but those have been destroyed by time. Outside, the stone chimney is split by a lightning bolt–shaped crevice. The ruins of an old well sit in the front yard, and the surrounding land includes remnants of an old barn and outhouse.

You can almost imagine a time when Anthony Cole and his family lived on this land. He had fourteen children and at least eighteen grandchildren, as well as tons of nieces and nephews. His large family owned hundreds of acres along the Eno River.

Remains of many of their mills and homesteads can still be found today in the Few's Ford area of the Eno River State Park. Just down the way, a small, squat cabin known as Sister's House is another favorite of photographers and historians.

Sadly, despite being one of the Eno community's most prominent families, history has not been kind to the Cole family. "Then came the 'Durham sickness,' typhoid from contaminated wells, which killed the Coles and others mercilessly. In 1908 their mills were washed away by the hundred year flood. Their lands are now diminished by Durham's development," wrote Eno historian Margaret Nygard, who played a major role in preserving the history of the land and fighting to protect it from being flooded.

Even though they are gone, the remaining ruins of the Cole family's homestead are a powerful contribution to understanding the history of the Eno River community.

The Cabelands

Along another section of river is the homestead of John Cabe and his family, with ruins including the stony remains of an old mill and a cemetery with many unmarked graves.

John Cabe settled along the Eno River in the late 1700s. According to Nygard, if Anthony Cole was the "Patriarch of the Eno," then John Cabe was the "Abraham of the Eno," the "head of a mill oligarchy on the

Opposite: A faded gravestone hidden in the Cabelands. Dozens of unmarked graves rest in these woods. *Courtesy of Kelly Gomez,* The Forgotten South.

The stone remains of John Cabe's mill, found in the Cabelands along the Eno River. He settled here in the 1700s. *Courtesy of Kelly Gomez,* The Forgotten South.

rivers of the region." During a time when women could not typically own property, and therefore would struggle to gain personal wealth, Cabe had nine daughters. To protect their futures, but likely also to ensure his family's lineage and wealth, he utilized the political power of marriage. "It was not a little singular that each of the men his daughters married all owned a merchant mill," wrote Nygard.

Today, the site of his family's homestead is known colloquially as the Cabelands, and it has a reputation of eerie happenings and spooky legends that comes out in stories each October. Not nearly as many ruins survived along his stretch of the Eno as you might find on Cole's property; however, a sizable remnant from one of Cabe's older mills can still be found crumbling deep in the trench of the old millrace.

His family cemetery can also be found in the woods, partially obscured by overgrowth. Many hikers walk right past without even noticing. Of more than fifty grave sites in the cemetery, only twelve have markers remaining. It's likely that at some point each family member's burial plot was lovingly marked with a headstone; however, centuries have not been kind to the Cabelands.

Saving the Eno

Centuries of history could have been washed away along the Eno River Valley, creating an "underwater ghost town." Fortunately, a group of activists and historians stood before Durham City Council in the 1960s to strongly oppose the plan to build a dam on the river to bolster the city's water supply.

There are many underwater ghost towns across North Carolina; almost every man-made lake has flooded centuries of history, and despite lawsuits and pushback, no one was able to prevent it from happening. Durham had already utilized the Eno as a water supply in the past; the ruins of the pump station remain on the shore to prove it. It seems obvious they would want to use the natural resource that had been supplying local communities for generations. It therefore seems almost miraculous that the Eno River State Park exists today with history intact.

In August 1966 Margaret Nygard led a group to speak out at the Durham City Council meeting. A few months later, the group formed the Association for Preservation of the Eno River Valley. They began digging into the history of the valley, uncovering historic ruins, creating maps, scheduling tours of the sites, and presenting their important history. They even told chilling ghost stories—like the ghost of the Cabelands haunting the old millrace. Hundreds of people began attending their events.

By 1972, after teaming up with The Nature Conservancy, they received an endorsement for acquiring property for a state park, as well as a donation of their first ninety acres. One year later, the Eno River State Park was officially born.

Nygard didn't stop there. More than twenty years later, a 1995 article in the *Durham Herald-Sun* showed she was pursuing more acreage for the park. Even more recently, in 2025, the park announced it had officially acquired the Occoneechee Speedway. Even today, the Eno River Association works diligently to preserve historic sites, protect the land, and keep the stories of the Eno River Valley alive.

Chapter 7

MILLBROOK VILLAGE

Little Village Swallowed by a Big City

I actually grew up in the fading embers of a dying village—and until I became a historian, I never even realized it. That's just how easy it is to lose history. One generation grew up in a community known as Millbrook; then, a blip later, their grandchildren forgot it ever existed.

To me, Millbrook was just a name on a street sign. I grew up near the intersection of Millbrook Road and Falls of Neuse Road. I went to school at Millbrook Elementary. My mom grew up in Millbrook, and my grandmother moved to Millbrook in the 1960s. But even surrounded by the name "Millbrook," I didn't realize I lived in a lost community.

No. I lived in Raleigh, our state's capital.

That's because by the 1980s, the blossoming city of Raleigh was overflowing into the surrounding area, swallowing up the little villages and rural communities that once existed around the city. However, as little as a century prior, the little village of Mill Brook shows up on the Wake County map, built along Marsh Creek and the Raleigh and Gaston Railroad. Nearby, the 1871 map shows several other mills, like Whitaker Mill and Harp's Mill, that have also vanished, magically transformed into modern-day street names.

How many thousands of locals drive along Millbrook Road each day, never realizing it once connected to a quaint little village with a tiny white post office, a historic school, a general store, a cotton gin, and even a sawmill that were central to a surrounding community of dairy farmers and a deeply religious way of life?

Hearts Delight was a beloved local ice cream shop that stood within the last remaining section of Historic Millbrook in the 1980s. *Courtesy of Randy Scherr.*

Located about six miles outside Raleigh, the agrarian village grew around the railroad and mills. Like many rural communities, much of the history is lost because, as one ninety-year-old farmer told me, "Farmers don't sit around writing about their own history." While plenty of history is written about the nearby cities, it's so easy to lose the history of our small towns—the stories that make up the very backbone of our state.

Very little remains of the original Millbrook Village today—but there are a few secret remnants if you know where to find them. Those secret spaces are full of stories.

The Original Mill Brook: Crumbling Ruin Hidden in Suburbia

You never know what hidden history may be buried in your own backyard—and there's one specific yard in Raleigh that may hold the origin point of Millbrook Village.

Tucked away in a neighborhood not far from Millbrook High School is an unusual stone structure: a wall of granite stones spanning roughly twenty-five feet across a peaceful creek, towering around twelve feet tall over a smooth, flat stone base. Very few people even know about the hidden relic, but those who do all say the same thing: It's been there as long as anyone can remember.

Jack Norwood, born and raised in Millbrook Village for almost one hundred years, recalls having picnics with his grandfather on the flat rock beneath the wall. That was during the 1930s. His grandfather, reaching deep into memories, said the mill was a ruin even as far back as the late 1800s.

"He told me about the wall," said Jack. "He told me it was the original Mill Brook."

A stone wall hidden in a neighborhood off Falls of Neuse Road in Raleigh. It's believed to be the original mill brook. *Author's personal collection.*

The remains of the old mill are hidden in the backyard of a private residence. Jack Norwood, who has lived in Millbrook nearly a century, remembers having picnics here growing up—and it was just a ruin even then. *Author's personal collection.*

That smooth flat rock in the pool of water at the end of the creek?

"That was the millpond," he said. "The stone wall was the dam."

As with many 1800s mills, the creek likely formed a waterfall over the dam wall, forming the smooth stone that now sits at its base. Nearby, a telltale trench running across the landscape likely served as the stream overflow channel. The current property owner has also found the sluice, as well as old rusty parts scattered around their yard. Chunks of old bricks litter the waterway.

While doing research on the mill several years ago, I invited a representative from the Office of State Archaeology to take a look at the wall. He confirmed it appeared to have been a mill, and based on "plug-and-feather" markings on each stone, he could deduce the stones were quarried in the 1800s.

Based on its location, age, and oral history, it seems likely this is the original Mill Brook that the surrounding village was built around.

It seems a miracle any part of the old mill survived this long. Nowadays, Marsh Creek is relatively small and quiet. However, the family who owns the land says during heavy rains, the creek turns into a deluge that floods their backyard.

Just as the mill ruins have survived the torrents of nature, they've also survived generations of erosion—not from water but from the soles of children's shoes. As recently as the 1970s, kids who grew up in the neighborhood recall playing on the mysterious stone wall, using it as a fort or a perfect picnic spot. Some kids remembered tying a rope to a tree branch and swinging from the top of the mill wall or sliding down the slippery, wet stones.

I wonder if the original mill owners, using the structure for life-sustaining sustenance, could ever envision a time when their grand community mill would be a forgotten ruin—so unrecognizable that the surrounding neighborhood no longer even realized its original importance.

While oral history maintains this stone ruin is the original Mill Brook, historians have never been able to 100 percent confirm the wall's origins. Because of the lack of written history, there's still a lot of mystery surrounding the old structure.

When was the mill built? Who built the mill? Who were the original owners? What exactly did this mill produce? How was it destroyed—was it a fire or flood, or was it intentionally torn down? What happened to the millstone? Did it suffer the fate of so many other mills—washed away in a hurricane that caused Marsh Creek to swell? Burned down by a flickering candle gone astray?

If we let the memories of Millbrook Village vanish into the mouth of North Raleigh, we may never solve the mysteries of the old Millbrook.

Living on Faith: Church Becomes Central to Millbrook Village

Millbrook Village began as a small community of family farms and mills several miles north of Raleigh, which experienced rapid growth in the 1860s when it became the first stop north of the capital along the Raleigh and Gaston Railroad.

Once the railroad station was complete, a little village formed along the tracks. It grew by the 1880s to include a few businesses, a post office, merchant shops, and even some homes that offered rooms for travelers. A larger railroad depot was built as the community expanded. Millbrook became the first stop for trains headed north out of Raleigh.

Millbrook Village was a community deeply invested in faith, with church being central to their lives. "In the early days, the farming families traveled on Sundays to gather at the nearest church: New Hope Baptist or Mount Vernon Baptist," explained Dru McClelland Smith, a member for nearly fifty years at Millbrook Baptist Church, one of the community's earliest churches. "But as Millbrook's population grew, the hardworking farmers wanted a closer place to gather, so they wouldn't have to travel as far on Sundays."

The surrounding area consisted of large farms, roughly fifty to one hundred acres each, meaning nobody lived close to one another, and everyone had to travel to reach the "main stretch" of town with the railroad station, cotton gin, general store, and mills. Managing the large farms kept folks busy with chores, and it became demanding to travel so far each weekend to attend church.

To save time on travel, faithful farming families began meeting in a nearby brush arbor, rather than making the lengthy trip to either Mount Vernon or New Hope, which were the nearest church buildings at the time.

"A brush arbor or grape arbor is like a little outdoor gathering place," explained Smith. "That's where our congregation first began meeting. There were only around fifteen people."

Artistic renderings depict brush arbors as an outdoor garden area, sometimes with wooden benches or simple seating, surrounded by green hedges and beneath the shade of a grapevine. "Our brush arbor was where North Ridge Shopping Center is today," said Smith. Thousands of people shop there each year, never realizing they're walking over the sacred ground where Millbrook Baptist Church began.

"The first preachers arrived on horseback or by buggy, coming from Wake Forest or Raleigh," she said. "They were traveling preachers."

Church members pointed me to an old house hidden in the woods off Falls of Neuse Road, saying that's where traveling preachers would stay while they were in town. Traveling preachers often arrived on Friday night and stayed through the weekend. In those early days, church services rotated on a farming schedule, allowing time for families to manage their crop schedule. Services were held on Saturday afternoons and Sunday mornings once a month.

A painting of the historic Millbrook Baptist Church, which has been serving Millbrook for 150 years. *Courtesy of Millbrook Baptist Church.*

Just like farmwork, church meetings had seasonal schedules. Revival meetings were held for a full week in August. An excerpt from a history of Millbrook Baptist describes those early worship services, saying:

> *Summer farm work was over and harvest had not yet begun, so farmers were free to attend all day services with "dinner on the grounds," which meant long, improvised tables, laden with food—with cooks striving to outdo one another with their culinary efforts. The long, hot afternoon services were often trying after the big, noon-day meal. However hard on the cooks and farmers, everyone looked forward to the summer meetings of renewal of faith and friendships. Often in the long, cold winter, roads were too bad for horse and buggy travel, and families remained at home for worship.*

By 1875, the little outdoor congregation had outgrown its brush arbor. A man named Elias K. Chappell donated land at the corner of Spring Forest Road and Falls of Neuse Road. A new church was built and dubbed Midway Baptist Church because of its location "midway" between the other two churches.

In 1920, the congregation voted to move to a "more favorable" location just down the road into the bustling village of Millbrook. They began hosting meetings in the Millbrook School while they built a new sanctuary on land obtained from J.B. Green. In 1924, they held their first church service in the new building and changed their name to Millbrook Baptist Church.

"In those days, Millbrook was still so small and rural. We had a post office, a store, a cotton gin, and a few homes near the school," described Smith.

In 1924, Reverend J.S. Farmer began a fourteen-year pastorate that had such a profound impact on the church it's still remembered a century later. "His home was built where Quail Ridge Apartments are today," said Smith. That's just a stone's throw away from the remains of the old mill.

That historic sanctuary stood like a sentinel on Millbrook Road for decades—even as the world changed around it, even as Millbrook Road was extended and widened until the busy lanes almost touched the sanctuary's doorstep. Raleigh was growing, starting to devour the once tiny village. Eventually, the widened road pushed the congregation to build a new building. Over time, the historic sanctuary became too expensive to maintain and was torn down. However, the church bell and a piece of the original steeple were saved and are on display today.

The churches of Millbrook have become the keepers of the village's history, with very little of the original village remaining outside of the historic sanctuaries and their documents. Well into the final days of Millbrook Village, the church remained central to the community—with faded photos of church potlucks and Christmas programs serving as the village archives and memories of church leaders and Sunday school teachers serving as the village's historic icons.

In 2025, Millbrook Baptist Church celebrated its 150th anniversary. As part of the celebration, the congregation delved into old photos and stories to ensure the century and a half of history is passed along to the next generation of members.

The Women Who Built Millbrook

Church was central to life in Millbrook Village, so decisions made in the local churches had ripple effects on the entire community. When the church began allowing women into leadership roles in the early 1900s—a somewhat unconventional decision for the era—it left a major impression on the ladies of Millbrook. Some might even say that impression has lasted until the modern day.

Records show that it was around 1905 when Fannie Heck, a social activist and leader of the Baptist Woman's Missionary Union, began calling on women in nearby churches to organize missionary societies. Heck lived in the historic Heck-Andrews house on Blount Street in the neighboring city of Raleigh.

Some of the women who served at Millbrook Baptist Church have created ripple effects lasting generations, becoming like folk heroes of historic Millbrook Village.

Among these women were Mrs. Eugene Beddingfield, Mrs. Sam Harp, and Mrs. Sanderford—three surnames that appear throughout Millbrook Village's history. Mrs. Beddingfield's husband served as postmaster. Later, Reverend Farmer's wife stepped into the role leading the Missionary Society.

"The Millbrook ladies were in awe of his wife," said Smith. "She was a former missionary to Japan. Her family were educators and college presidents. She was a strong church leader and held weekly group meetings for women in missions."

According to archival details shared by Millbrook Baptist Church, "The husbands, who were having to look after the children while their wives were meeting, peeped in the doors with wondering looks as to what the ladies could be doing for so long a time."

Another woman well-remembered by the church is Mary B. Green, who was often seen carrying armloads of books from the library to deliver them to Sunday school classes and missionary meetings. Today, the library carries her name.

In more recent years, there's another woman whose name and memory live on the lips of nearly every member of Millbrook Baptist Church: Gloria Norwood and her husband, Jack. Not only did they take on leadership roles within the church, but their historic home and farm—a time capsule from the old days of Millbrook Village—became a gathering place for community activities.

Norwood Farm: A Time Capsule Protected from Developers

If you look at a bird's-eye view of North Raleigh, you'll see miles of modern development—parking lots, shopping centers, intersections—surrounding a

Artist's rendition of Jack Norwood's farm, which has been part of Millbrook for more than a century. *Author's personal collection.*

small island of green hidden in the hustle-bustle. That little green oasis is a sanctuary of old Millbrook, untouched by a century's worth of growth and modernization that devoured the rural village after it was annexed by

Raleigh. This time capsule is Jack Norwood's farm. He has lived here for almost one hundred years.

Before that, his father and grandfather also roamed the roads of historic Millbrook Village back in the 1800s, when it was a burgeoning farm and railroad community. Photos from early Millbrook showcase a simple life, with hunched old farmers smiling in a dirt-carpeted barnyard, posing alongside free-roaming chickens in front of a sagging wooden coop. One photo shows a couple of men in floppy hats standing next to a couple of dead hogs dangling from a wooden beam.

Jack's farm is like seeing these antique black-and-white photos come to life in full color: a bright red barn against a blue sky, sitting on the horizon of a rolling green field with a dirt path curling around it. Frames of dusty wooden outbuildings—some in shambles—shelter old farming equipment. A painting on the wall inside his home depicts a familiar scene: Jack, his profile easily recognizable, riding a tractor through his fields.

Who knows how long it's been since Jack was able to use the tractor?

Even today, those Raleigh and Gaston Railroad tracks cut through his land—a reminder of the village's origins.

According to an architectural survey by historian Ruth Little in 1992, the Norwood farm was one of only a handful of farms in Wake County that maintained enough acreage to still be considered historic farms.

"Onnis Norwood, who was born in north Wake County, established his fifty-four-acre farm near the community of Millbrook north of Raleigh in the 1930s. Onnis grew cotton, tobacco, hay, and corn. His mule barn and numerous other frame buildings still stand on the property. To supplement his agricultural income, he operated a lumber mill on the farm."

Jack remembers the lumber mill. It was called Norwood Brothers and was managed by him and his three brothers.

"We had a sawmill on the edge of the property," he said. "The train would come by, and we'd load it up with lumber."

The mill closed up shop in 1972.

However, the Norwood farm took on another important role in the Millbrook community. Instead of being a center for Millbrook's agriculture and lumber, it became a center for Millbrook's faith and religion.

Smith remembers a time, not so long ago, when the Norwood Farm hosted church gatherings—and at least one wedding—beneath the protective branches of a beautiful, ancient tree.

"It was so magnificent," she recalled. "And Gloria, his wife, had the most beautiful garden."

Artist's rendition of Jack Norwood riding his tractor around on the family farm. A portrait of days gone by. *Author's personal collection.*

"She had acres of flowers, and she would go out into her field on the farm and trim them to create personalized arrangements to decorate church," she recalled, smiling. "And crowds would gather at the Norwood farm in the morning to buy her fresh-cut flowers. You had to get there early if you wanted the full selection. She sold them all so quickly."

Gloria was so passionate about her role in the community and church that she decided to attend seminary in Wake Forest under a well-known Bible scholar. "Just to make sure she was teaching the Bible correctly," said Smith. "Dates, timelines, people—she just made it come alive in her lessons."

Gloria knew which translation of the Bible each and every one of her members had. "If you were not in class, it was a guarantee you could expect a note in the mail saying you were missed and hoping you'd be back the following Sunday. She'd even send you a scripture to read," said Smith. "She made even the smallest things so special."

Jack and Gloria are remembered as being humble and quiet—a reflection of the humble beginnings of the small, rural Millbrook Village.

"Jack was soft-spoken, but when he spoke, you knew it was going to be meaningful," said Smith. "And Gloria. She was such a gentle woman. I remember her with her long hair, wisped up into a soft bun. She wore plain, simple dresses. Neither of them were flashy."

In time, the Norwood farm became one of the only tangible remnants of Historic Millbrook. How meaningful that more than a century after the church began, they still found a way to congregate in the only remaining piece of their original hometown.

The Final Days of Millbrook Village

It may be strange to imagine, but some locals remember a time before the bustling shopping centers and malls brought clogging traffic to modern-day Capital Boulevard. Instead, longtime locals like Jack Norwood and Evelyn Stevens recall a time when green pastures and dairy farms sat at the intersection with Spring Forest Road.

"Even in the 1950s and '60s, it was still country, country, country," said Norwood.

"It was before North Hills. Before Crabtree," added Stevens. "We had to drive all the way to Cameron Village or Five Points just to get groceries."

Stevens recalled a row of teeny old houses, now long gone, that once stood along Falls of Neuse Road. "You just wouldn't believe what it looked like then," she recalled.

Down by modern-day Eastgate Park was a cow pasture and a farmer who lived in a log cabin. Local kids would go play in the creek.

"Capital Boulevard was farms. There was even a tunnel built underneath the road so the cows could go back and forth," said Norwood. "Lots of farms, and old stores like Mr. Honeycutt's and Mr. Hatch's."

In those days, they still called it Millbrook—not Raleigh.

The iconic deck of Hearts Delight, an ice cream shop that brought fun and flavor to the final days of Historic Millbrook. *Courtesy of Randy Scherr.*

Stevens says it was the merging of Wake County Public Schools in 1976 that really spelled the end of Historic Millbrook. "When city schools and country schools merged, we had a really big surge of people who moved out here from the city," she said.

By the 1970s and '80s, many of the remnants of Historic Millbrook Village were starting to fade. The original mill, the old shops, the cotton gin—gone, replaced by rapid growth and expansion of shopping centers and neighborhoods along Millbrook Road. Even the tiny, iconic white post office, decaying along the roadside for so many years, was long gone.

However, some recall, as late as the 1980s, a little brown wooden sign outside a popular ice cream shop. It read "Historic Millbrook."

Part of that final surviving vestige of old Millbrook was a beloved ice cream shop known as Hearts Delight. Outside, the building had a unique, historic appearance—like something from an old-timey village. Inside, it was bursting with literally thousands of hearts. Each year, owner Randy Scherr hosted a popular celebrity scoop for the surrounding neighborhoods.

"And we had a special flavor," he recalled. "Old-fashioned vanilla, topped with cinnamon hearts."

Kids born in the 1980s in the last days of Millbrook may have Hearts Delight as their final taste of Millbrook history. For me, personally, that little building with the "Historic Millbrook" sign, mixed with the taste of blue bubblegum ice cream, is the only memory of Millbrook I have.

But for people like Jack Norwood, who has lived in Millbrook for nearly a century on a family farm that's somehow remained untouched by Raleigh's developers, those memories are all he's ever known. "It was a different time. It was a different world," said Norwood. "Time goes by."

Chapter 8

HENRY RIVER MILL VILLAGE

Keeping a Ghost Town Alive

After years of preservation work, one of the most famous, beautiful and visually intact ghost towns in North Carolina faces an uncertain future.

Even if you've never visited, it's likely that you've seen Henry River Mill Village. Abandoned decades ago, this humble mill community has enjoyed national attention on multiple platforms—television shows, documentaries, magazines, newspapers, and books. Its striking dystopian visuals provided an iconic backdrop for scenes in *The Hunger Games* movie.

Curious urban explorers have been drawn to its haunting beauty ever since the last resident was forced to leave, sometime between the late 1990s and early 2000s. After years of battling with trespassers and vandals, new owners eventually opened the entire village for tours. Guests could even stay the night in a renovated millhouse.

Since opening for public tours, Henry River Mill Village has become most people's best chance to wander through a mostly intact ghost town, strolling through acres of beauty and decay—a snapshot of the simplicity and struggles of life in a southern Appalachian mill town built at the turn of the century.

Somehow, the charmed and famous Henry River Mill Village has thus far avoided the fate of so many ghost towns and lost communities in the Old North State—many of which have been wiped off the map, destroyed by circumstances, leaving unrecognizable piles of rubble and stones where homes once stood.

Built in 1905 and abandoned decades ago, Henry River Mill Village is one of the most intact ghost towns in North Carolina. *Author's personal collection.*

How has this humble mill village managed to avoid the desolate fate of so many ghost towns?

"The biggest part was our sense of community," recalled Anita Brittain, who was born to bloom in the soil of Henry River. "We were all a family. All of us were co-workers, neighbors, family. We didn't always have much, but we shared what we did have. The people that grew up here appreciated life and learned to always try and help others."

Decades after the last person was forced to leave their house in Henry River, the former residents still refused to give up on their home.

"My dad still went back to our home almost every day, even after he was forced to move out," recalled Brittain. "He'd sit on the front porch each day. He'd tidy up the yard. And other former residents knew he'd be there, so they'd walk past and chat with him, sometimes bring him some tomatoes."

Brittain was just one of many volunteers who continually visited their old homes, cleaning and cutting back foliage, refusing to allow the empty town to be swallowed by the hungry maw of Mother Nature.

"We volunteered for years. Cleaned it up and made it really look good," she said. "The state really helped a lot. The owners were wonderful, too."

With so many visitors and so much historic interest, it seemed the future of Henry River Mill Village was stable—until a real estate listing in late 2024 struck fear into the hearts of locals. Their beloved village was for sale.

"It just broke my heart," said Brittain, her voice thick.

Who will buy the property, and what will they do with it? Will a preservation-minded owner take over and continue allowing tours and renovations? Will a developer see value in the land, but not the decaying structures, and tear it all down?

The future is anyone's guess.

Take a Step Back in Time: Exploring Henry River Mill Village Today

Just one glance at Henry River Mill Village, and you can see just how that rich Appalachian soil grew and sustained such a kind, humble, and hardworking community.

More than a dozen of the original thirty-five millhouses are still standing, creating neat rows on either side of the main road. A peek through broken windows reveals simple but cozy living rooms, some with dust-covered furniture still frozen in time. You could almost imagine a family full of children gathered around the fireplace after a long day at the mill.

Central to the village skyline is a tall brick general store with whitewashed double doors and faded lettering beneath windowpanes: "Pastries. Cakes." The homemade sweets in Henry River Mill Village were reportedly second-to-none.

A short hike down to the river reveals the remnants of a textile mill that once struck an imposing and grand figure on the riverbank.

The white paint that once gleamed on the brand-new homes has long since peeled off, leaving behind the ruddy brown of the original wood. Overgrown ivy creeps up the siding, providing natural curtains for the hollowed-out windows. The yards are grassy and wide, with ancient trees still standing guard, and you can imagine children playing games outside together while the women hang laundry in the sun to dry or work in their gardens, growing fresh vegetables and colorful flowers.

Brittain doesn't have to imagine. She lived it.

Henry River Mill Village in its heyday. Compare with how it looks today. *Courtesy of Anita Brittain and Henry River Mill Village.*

She sees all those wooden porches—many with rotting floorboards beginning to cave in—and remembers long summer evenings when the grown-ups would sit on the porches talking while the kids played games beneath the streetlights.

"We'd play games until it was so dark," she smiled. "It was them enjoying themselves, and they'd give us some time to enjoy ourselves."

During the weekday afternoons, those same porches were full of children, hanging out and working on homework together so they could go play.

"We did everything together," she said. "We had to do our chores and our homework, and then we'd all go play together. We were always together. If one of us got in trouble, we all got in trouble."

The crew of Henry River kids would go off on free-roaming adventures, playing games or running to the ballfield. There was also a big grassy area near the textile mill where kids would gather to play.

"It might be dark before we got home. But our parents didn't worry; we were all together, and it felt like a family," she said.

Brittain lived on the main road, where many of the houses remain standing today, along a sharp curve that leads to the general store. Her home is still there—the one she and her youngest sister were born in. The one they lived in until they got married and moved away in 1970. Even then, her children would go back and visit all the time, spending time with their grandma and grandpa on the weekend.

"My dad was one of the last ones to leave the village," said recalled. "The only reason he left was because the county came in and said they had to empty the houses because there was no running water except outside. There was no indoor bathrooms or anything, even at that time."

With wooden outhouses, sweltering summers, bitter cold winters, homegrown food, and a job at the mill, certainly the small millhouses weren't palaces. Some families were better off than others, and they would often share their excess with neighbors. No one was going to become wealthy in Henry River Mill Village. Brittain's father had been working the mill since before 1930, with some restrictions on what he could do because he was a child. Not everyone learned how to read, although this village reportedly had a higher literacy rate than many others.

"Even though we didn't have everything that a lot of other people may have had—who thought they were so rich—but I think we were richer." recalled Brittain. "Because we had each other. I had a brother and three sisters, but honestly the other kids were all my siblings, too. I counted them that way. I felt like I had a whole lot of extra mommies and daddies."

Those deep roots of community and love are probably why Henry River Mill Village is still in such good shape.

"There's more to life than just schooling," said Brittain, who is herself a retired teacher. "There's living life and being there for each other. It was a good life. We were loved. And that makes a lot of difference. I wouldn't change it for anything."

Church, Education, and Everyday Life in an Early 1900s Mill Village

There was a time when mill villages were commonplace along the waterways of North Carolina. In the 1800s, mills were the backbone of the town economy. You needed lumber mills to build houses, cotton mills to make

Step back in time: the old general store at Henry River Mill Village. *Courtesy of Anita Brittain and Henry River Mill Village.*

clothes, gristmills to grind your food. Some mills were small, just large enough to support the surrounding community. Others were industrial mills that brought in wealth from multiple surrounding areas.

Mill work was difficult and dangerous, and enduring child labor laws were not yet in place until the late 1930s. Wages were sometimes so low that workers would go on strike, and sometimes the entire family would have to work in order to make enough scratch to get by. Conditions were harsh, dry, and hot, and the demanding workday would last up to twelve hours.

Just as castles in Europe often had a small town surrounding them, industrial mills often had a small mill village connected to them. Employees would be assigned a house to live in, and life completely revolved around the mill. Often, the entire town was owned by the mill—including the shops, homes, and churches—so a good mill owner could mean a more stable life, and a severe mill owner could mean the challenges of the workday bled over into every aspect of your daily life.

Education in a Rural Mill Village

According to newspaper articles from 1919, Henry River Mill Village was a unique community with exceptionally beautiful houses and happy home lives. The Aderholdt family, who owned the village and mill, had set out to create a clean and comfortable community. Instead of working all day in the mill, some of the children were able to attend school, and many of the families, illiterate when they arrived, were afforded opportunities to learn to read.

Brittain recalls her uncle using the upstairs of the old general store for a schoolhouse, where he would help teach mill workers to read.

"My dad, I don't think he went to that. But he went to fifth grade, and there was no math problem I've ever seen that he couldn't work. He taught us a lot of things in our home," she said.

Like many village students, Brittain went to Hildebran for high school and graduated in 1962. She then went to Lenoir-Rhyne University in Hickory. Eventually, her path brought her back to Hildebran, where she taught the next generation of Henry River kids.

"I taught a lot of the children of the people that I grew up with. Or their grandkids," she said.

Church and Community

The *Charlotte Observer* described the people of Henry River Mill Village in 1919, writing, "They are a rugged type of mountain folk, great believers in pure home life and intensely religious."

Church was a big part of life and culture in many rural mill villages. One of Brittain's earliest memories from her youngest days involves walking to church with her family: "I was real small. We walked to church, and I remember Dad walking us home. We come down and around the old road. We go down around the houses and come through the field. A lot of families would all be walking that same path together to and from church."

Growing up, Brittain was a member of Henry River Baptist Church, but it's changed a lot since she was a little girl. "It's brick and everything now," she said.

Before she was born, there was a smaller church behind the ballfield, but it burned down, and the Aderholdt family provided land for the new church. In the earliest days, the people of Henry River gathered in the general store for church services, just as they did for school.

"We also had preachers who would visit and do cottage prayer meetings at different houses in the village," she said.

Brittain fondly remembers the church offering a girls' group program that she describes as similar to Girl Scouts. "We'd rotate meeting at different homes, and the moms would provide a snack and some juice. We'd do projects and sometimes go out on field trips," she recalled. "And to raise money for the church, we'd sell these Dolly Does-It scrubbers. Just about everyone had one, and of all the items I've saved from the village over the years, I really wish I had one of those! They were so useful!"

Despite any hardships of life in a mill village at the turn of the century, Brittain still described life in one word: community. The community was tightknit. You didn't have neighbors or co-workers; you had family.

"There was a family who lived on the Hill, and they'd often go without groceries. I know many times my mom and dad went to the general store and bought food for them," she said. "Life was just simple then. We just helped one another, and we appreciated life. We had some good people living in Henry River Mill Village. Hardworking. And generous with anything we had."

Family and Teammates: Community on the Ballfield

Family. Neighbors. Co-workers. There are a lot of words to describe the community at Henry River Mill Village.

There is another really important word they often used: teammates.

Pretty much anyone who grew up in Henry River Mill Village will share memories of the old ballfield. Softball and baseball were a major part of life for both kids and adults.

Brittain remembers her dad playing on the Henry River Mill team against other local mills like Long View and Grand Falls. Kids also had their own teams, both boys and girls. "Guess who was the pitcher on the girls' softball team?" grinned Brittain. "At the time, girls' teams were hard to come by. We'd play against church teams and other nearby groups."

First, children had to help with chores and do their schoolwork. They'd gather together on someone's porch, sweating in the shade on those hot days of a North Carolina summer, practicing their lessons until it was finally time to go play.

"Most of the time if it was summer, we were at the ballfield," recalled Brittain. "If the boys were playing, the girls were there to watch them. And if the girls played, the boys were there to watch them."

The general store at Henry River Mill Village today. Compare it with how it looked decades ago. *Author's personal collection.*

On nights when the boys', girls', or mill teams weren't playing on the local ballfield, her dad would take them to watch professional baseball. "He'd gather up a bunch of us kids on the Hill, and we'd take off to the ballgames in Hickory. We'd go to Rebel games. We'd go to American Legion games," she said. "Even if Dad didn't plan on going that night, my brother could talk to him and convince him—and off we'd all go!"

One memory that sticks with her reminds her what a strong community they had. "He'd often take other kids who didn't have a dad of their own," she said.

Just like he loved sitting on his old front porch once Henry River Mill Village was vacated, her dad also loved baseball. When he passed away, her father was the longest season ticket holder for the Hickory Crawdads team.

"It was just a real sense of community. It was really like a family. Even today, many of these families who played ball together are still close," she said. "And I've got some of the best memories."

Why Was Henry River Mill Village Abandoned?

In its heyday, Henry River Mill Village was a place full of hardworking families and a reportedly kind and compassionate owner who prioritized education, church, and recreation to keep residents happy and healthy. The large textile mill and comfortable homes made Henry River a desirable place to live and work.

Despite rapid growth and success at the Henry River Mill through the 1960s, the textile industry began losing steam overall, and mills were no longer the economic driver they once had been.

The mill ceased operations by the 1970s, and in 1977, the property was bought by Wade Sheppard. Shortly after, the main mill burned to the ground.

After decades of resilience and community, Henry River Mill Village died a slow death, with families slowly trickling away one by one and leaving their homes behind. Nearby towns offered modern amenities like indoor

Guests can step back in time to explore a real mill village, peeking in windows to find furniture left behind. Guests can even stay the night. *Author's personal collection.*

plumbing. Even if one or two people remained in the village, it would have already seemed like a ghost town, drawing attention to vandals and urban explorers alike.

Owning a fully abandoned ghost town, the property owner was constantly having to scare off trespassers and vandals.

Brittain's father, one of the last people to leave the village, still hung around their family home for years after vacating. Together, the community worked together to protect and preserve the abandoned town. Eventually, new owners opened Henry River Mill Village for tours, and it began a renaissance, with guests flocking from around the country and Hollywood crews bringing it to life once again.

With the potential for new owners, Brittain and other locals are nervous about what's in store for their beloved home. There are examples of several historic mill villages in North Carolina that have been restored or maintained. Rocky Mount has transformed its large mill into modern apartments and office spaces, with the surrounding structures taken over by breweries, restaurants, and coffee shops. The mill village is being used as cozy housing. Likewise, McAdenville's downtown area still has the original mill housing, and the old mill still looks like a castle wall.

Henry River Mill Village, however, is the only mill village that remains untouched, with that ghost town veneer. Instead of a modern-day shopping center or neighborhood, it's maintained its original historic look.

While she waits to see what happens next, Brittain says some of the old millhouses are going down fast. She is still doing all she can to preserve the history of her hometown. She has started a social media group where people can share memories and photos. She's working with historians and authors to get the story into books. She even collected cultural recipes from the people of Henry River to make sure those old Appalachian flavors she grew up with won't vanish forever.

Just as her mother and aunts grew gardens outside their cottages in Henry River, Brittain keeps a garden outside her modern-day home. Growing here are flowers and plants transplanted from gardens in Henry River Mill Village—roots from the soil of her old home transplanted into new soil.

"When we moved out, we took some of the garden with us. My aunt had a whole row of Easter lilies. I have peonies. A lilac bush. Anytime a family member passed away or moved out from a Henry River house, I tried to go take a plant from their garden and plant it here."

Almost everyone in Henry River Mill Village had a garden. Now, a little piece of the community lives on right in her own home.

But honestly, from the stories she tells, it sounds like most of the Henry River community is still alive anyway—right in the hearts of all the former residents. That's why the ghost town has survived so long: They didn't want to give up on their home.

Still, Brittain is nervous for the future of the historic site. "I'd work so hard to be able to keep the village as close to what it was when I was growing up," she said somberly. "I just want people to have a chance to remember what it was—and what it stood for."

No one would likely imagine this simple little mill village was one of the wealthiest communities in North Carolina—wealthy with love, joy, generosity. But most of all, community.

"The houses and things may be gone, but the memories won't be," she said wistfully. "And I wouldn't trade those memories for nothing."

ACKNOWLEDGEMENTS

It's truly difficult to know who to thank first. Multiple loved ones made sacrifices of their time and put their own blood, sweat, and tears into ensuring this book would be completed. So all in one swoop, I'll thank—in no particular order—my mom, my dad, and my husband.

Exploring abandoned places hidden in the woods isn't always the safest adventure, so I'm grateful to my mom and husband for making sure I'd never have to go alone. They spent countless hours in the car, driving all across the state—from the mountains to the coast—so I could get photos of remote places. They trudged around in marshy coastal ghost towns and wore their aching legs to the bone hiking into the woods trying to find hidden homesteads. Thank you, Greg and Mom, for all the hours of travel and hiking you put into this book. And then, once we were home again, thank you for making me dinner and bringing me coffee on those long nights of writing and research.

To my dad, who is the reason I even have the opportunity to write about history. He is the one who first encouraged me to start exploring abandoned places and telling their stories and who first provided an outlet for me to begin publishing. On the website he provided for me, hundreds of thousands of people began reading about Hidden History. Thank you for instilling a love of history in me, for proofreading my work, for hours of phone calls to discuss more ideas, and for giving me the chance to live my dream of becoming a writer, storyteller, journalist, and historian.

Thank you to my friends. Amber, you believed in me before I did. Scoobies, you may not even realize it, but your encouragement has always helped keep me going when the road was long. Speaking of long roads: Vicki, you walked so many miles with me on our hunt for hidden history.

To my pup, Glimmer, who has traveled with me on every road trip and every hike and who, at the end of the day, warmed my feet while I wrote each chapter.

To my grandmother and my nana, who I know are watching right now. I wish you could see this book. To my grandpa, who liked every single history article I ever wrote.

To my writing teachers like Larry Fraller and Al Maginnes and my history teachers like Steven Kreis, Roger Payne, and Dennis Lundblad. I've always wanted to thank you in the acknowledgements section of my first book. Now I finally can!

To everyone I interviewed who got raw and emotional telling me stories of long-gone childhood homes they can never see again: I hope this book captures your story. Although we couldn't save the historic buildings, I at least hope I can save the stories from being forgotten.

To the history that is not yet destroyed—I hope this book encourages people to visit these ghost towns and lost communities and breathe life back into them.

To everyone who shared encouragement during those nights of burning the midnight oil, when my eyes were burning and I thought about giving up. Thank you for your kind words. They truly help more than you know.

As I did my research, I noticed one word popping up again and again: community. Every single one of these lost towns emphasized one thing above all else: the power of community.

So thank you to my community. Your stories and your support are the reason this book exists.

BIBLIOGRAPHY

Alamance County Deed Books. Alamance County Register of Deeds. Accessed online.

American Revolution Tour of N.C. "Dixon's Mill." AmRevNC.com.

Barefoot, Daniel W. *Touring North Carolina Revolutionary War Site.* John F. Blair, 1998.

Baskin, Yvonne. "On the Site of an Old Plantation: Soul City Black Capitalism." *News & Observer*, 1969.

Binkley, Johnny C. *Moonshiners & Revenuers: From Bootleggers to Arsonists, ATF's Battle Against Criminals in North Carolina.* Acclaim Press, 2020.

Brittain, Anita R. *Henry River Mill Village Food Culture: A Cookbook.* Redhawk Publications, 2019.

Burlington Daily Times-News. "Cane Creek to Dedicate New Church in Home-Coming and Anniversary Program Lasting All Day Sunday." September 30, 1942.

———. "Early History of Quakers Reviewed Up Through Sixteenth Century During Event at Cane Creek Church." October 9, 1942.

Charlotte Observer. "Good Health, Good Roads, and Good Schools—Three Good Things Run into Up at Henry River." January 3, 1919.

Daily Times-News (Burlington). "At Snow Camp Observance: Spirit of Early Settlers Is Lauded." June 24, 1963.

———. "Wilson Family Becomes Theatrical Dynasty at Snow Camp." August 7, 1987.

Dickinson, Patricia. "Friends Spring Meeting House National Register Nomination." 1986.

From Whence We Came: Cane Creek Meeting Sesquibicentennial Remembrance Book. Cane Creek Congregation, 2001.

Healy, Thomas. *Soul City: Race, Equality and the Lost Dream of an American Utopia.* Metropolitan Books, 2021.

Lawrence, Lee E. *The Lower Cape Fear in Colonial Days.* University of North Carolina Press, 1978.

Mason, Connie. "Portsmouth Remembered." Curated by Connie Mason.

McKee, Jim. *Brunswick Town and Fort Anderson State Historic Site.* Arcadia Publishing, 2021.

———. *Enough to Satisfy Every Man's Needs: Looking at the Development of Port Brunswick and the Lower Cape Fear Through an Environmental Lense.* Historical Lenses & Scholarship, 2015.

National Park Service. "Visiting Portsmouth Village—Cape Lookout National Seashore." NPS.com.

News & Observer. "New Hope Valley Residents Take Dim View of Moving." February 3, 1964.

Nichols, Rick. "Present at the Creation." *News & Observer*, 1973.

North Carolina Historical Highway Marker Program. "Cane Creek Meeting." www.ncmarkers.com.

Oliver, Duane. *Hazel Creek from Then Till Now.* N.p., 1989.

Pedlow, Franda D. *The Story of Brunswick Town.* Brunswick Town State Historic Site, 199?.

Regulator Papers, Colonial Records Vol. VII. North Carolina Department of Archives and History.

Rubes, Michael. "History of the Company Mill in Umstead Park." Friends of the Page-Walker, December 9, 2022. www.FriendsOfPageWalker.org.

Steddum, Janet. *Battle for Falls Lake.* N.p., 2007.

Teague, Bobbie. *Cane Creek: Mother of Meetings.* North Carolina Yearly Meeting of Friends, 1995.

U.S. Army Corps of Engineers. "Shadows from the Past: Twenty-Five Years of Archeological and Historical Investigations at the B. Everette Jordan Lake Project."

Wallace, Heather Leigh. *Images of America: Jordan Lake.* Arcadia Publishing, 2010.

Weber, Tom. *Stories in Stone: Memories from a Bygone Farming Community in North Carolina.* Umstead Coalition, 2004.

ABOUT THE AUTHOR

Heather Leah is a seventh-generation North Carolinian who believes in the power of storytelling and oral history to keep our state's memories alive. History is far more than what we find in books; it's the stories held by our elders, and we need to take time to listen and pass those stories down to future generations—or they'll be lost forever.

Her work uncovering hidden history has appeared in magazines, newspapers, and television programs across the country. She takes photos of everything she can because places that seem unassuming today will be lost history tomorrow. She believes in making history fun and engaging, approaching it like an adventure into an unknown world.

You can find more of her work on her website, HiddenHistorian.com.